Cambridge Elements

Elements in Ame
edited
Frances E. ___
Princeton University

THE DIMENSIONS AND IMPLICATIONS OF THE PUBLIC'S REACTIONS TO THE JANUARY 6, 2021, INVASION OF THE US CAPITOL

Gary C. Jacobson
University of California, San Diego

CAMBRIDGE
UNIVERSITY PRESS

Shaftesbury Road, Cambridge CB2 8EA, United Kingdom

One Liberty Plaza, 20th Floor, New York, NY 10006, USA

477 Williamstown Road, Port Melbourne, VIC 3207, Australia

314–321, 3rd Floor, Plot 3, Splendor Forum, Jasola District Centre,
New Delhi – 110025, India

103 Penang Road, #05–06/07, Visioncrest Commercial, Singapore 238467

Cambridge University Press is part of Cambridge University Press & Assessment,
a department of the University of Cambridge.

We share the University's mission to contribute to society through the pursuit of
education, learning and research at the highest international levels of excellence.

www.cambridge.org
Information on this title: www.cambridge.org/9781009495400

DOI: 10.1017/9781009495387

First published 2024

A catalogue record for this publication is available from the British Library.

ISBN 978-1-009-49540-0 Hardback
ISBN 978-1-009-49537-0 Paperback
ISSN 2515-1606 (online)
ISSN 2515-1592 (print)

The Dimensions and Implications of the Public's Reactions to the January 6, 2021, Invasion of the US Capitol

Elements in American Politics

DOI: 10.1017/9781009495387
First published online: April 2024

Gary C. Jacobson
University of California, San Diego

Author for correspondence: Gary C. Jacobson, gjacobson@ucsd.edu

Abstract The January 6, 2021, invasion of the US Capitol building by a mob trying to block certification of Joe Biden's victory attacked a bedrock principle of American democracy, the peaceful transfer of power following a presidential election. This Element describes how the public reacted to January 6 and situates these reactions in the broader context of contemporary American politics as well as the relevant political science literature. Section 1 reviews in detail public assessments of the invaders and their actions, Donald Trump's responsibility, and the House investigations as they evolved after January 6. Section 2 explores the origins, maintenance, and consequences of these opinions. It concludes by reviewing some broader implications of January 6 and its aftermath for the future health of American democracy.

Keywords: January 6 riots, Donald Trump, election denial, political violence, party polarization

ISBNs: 9781009495400 (HB), 9781009495370 (PB), 9781009495387 (OC)
ISSNs: 2515-1606 (online), 2515-1592 (print)

Contents

Introduction

On January 6, 2021, shortly after Donald Trump's address to a "Save America Rally" near the White House in which he rehashed his lie that the 2020 election had been stolen from him and demanded that the official results be set aside so that he could remain in office, a mob of his supporters invaded the Capitol building to stop Congress from formally certifying Joe Biden's victory. Some two thousand rioters broke through police lines and stormed through the doors, forcing members, their staffs, and Mike Pence and his family to flee into hiding. The attackers injured more than 140 police officers, three of whom died within days of strokes or heart attacks; four later committed suicide; one rioter was fatally shot while trying to break in past a barricaded door. The invaders vandalized offices, stole equipment, and spread feces in hallways. Their numbers included members of various far-right anti-government groups, including the Proud Boys, the Oath Keepers, and the Three Percenters, along with other assorted white supremacists, Christian nationalists, neo-Confederates, neo-Nazis, and QAnon devotees (H.R. Rep. No. 117–613, 2022: 499–530). However, a majority of those ultimately arrested for joining the insurrection had no group affiliation; they were ordinary, if unusually excitable, Trump supporters who shared with these fringe groups the "basic motivations of patriotism, anti-government, and the belief that the election was stolen" (Pape, 2022b: 4).

Some participants celebrated by posting selfies and videos from inside the building, taking obvious pride in what they were doing – and revealing their naiveté about what they had gotten themselves into, which turned out to be the Justice Department's biggest criminal investigation ever (Feuer, 2023a). As of January 2024, 1,248 people had been charged with crimes for their actions in the Capitol on January 6; 748 have pleaded guilty; only 3 of the 170 whose cases have gone to trial had been acquitted of all charges. Of the 764 sentenced so far, 64 percent had received prison time, with a median of 150 days and the longest at twenty-two years (NPR Staff, 2024).

The action on January 6 has been variously described as "an assault, a riot, an insurrection, domestic terrorism or even a coup attempt" (Bauder, 2021), but, by any definition, it was an unprecedented, violent attack on a bedrock principle of American democracy, the peaceful transfer of power following a presidential election. Yet in their own minds, the participants were not attacking American democracy but rather defending it from the threat posed by a stolen election, an illegitimate president, and a corrupt federal government (Pape, 2022b). The ultimate legacy of January 6 for American politics going forward will depend on how widely these beliefs are shared and, more broadly, how people come to view the January 6 actors and their actions. At first, the scenes from the Capitol seemed jarring enough to shake people out of their existing opinions and beliefs, particularly regarding

Trump, his big lie, and his apologists in Congress and elsewhere. For a brief time, this looked to be happening, but within a few weeks, the familiar partisan fault lines marking American politics during Trump's presidency reemerged almost intact. Since then, and despite the vivid and detailed depictions of the attack and surrounding events provided by a House committee's investigation in 2022, partisan divisions have only hardened. After the initial shock, reactions to January 6 have so far done more to feed than to counter the vicious cycle of mutual hostility and contempt between Americans who support and oppose Trump.

My purposes here are to describe how the public reacted to January 6 and to situate these reactions in the broader context of contemporary American politics as well as the relevant political science literature. In Section 1, I lay out the contours of public opinion regarding the events of January 6 and their aftermath in considerable detail, highlighting systematic patterns in the data. The most consequential finding is the prevalence and persistence of demonstrably false beliefs that comprise or shape the responses of most ordinary Republicans and Trump voters to polling questions about the events. I also consider the extent to which these responses are sincere rather than merely "expressive."

Section 2 examines the origins, maintenance, and consequences of the patterns identified in Section 1. I begin by noting how Donald Trump successfully cultivated a large and loyal following by voicing the grievances and antipathies of disaffected conservative whites, maligning the mainstream news media, and vilifying his Democratic opponents. His effective evocation of shared identities has left many of his supporters immune to unfavorable information about him, resorting to standard modes of motivated reasoning in the face of any potentially disturbing news. I also note how Republican political elites and right-wing media entrepreneurs, pursuing Trump's MAGA (Make America Great Again) followers in search of votes and profits, were happy to deliver congenial messages to the misinformed. I then consider some consequences of public responses to the events of January 6 for electoral politics in 2022, the shape of the Republican coalition, polarized partisanship, and reactions to Trump's multiple indictments in 2023, which promise to dominate electoral politics in 2024. I finish by considering the broader implications and legacy of January 6 for the current health of American democracy.

1 The Polling Data

1.1 Introduction

In this section, I review the results of hundreds of surveys that have probed various dimensions of the public's reactions to the Capitol invasion, beginning immediately after the event and continuing through the House Select Committee's hearings in June and July 2022, its *Final Report* issued in December, and through the end of 2023.[1] These surveys have investigated, in diverse ways, the three main areas of public opinion on the events of January 6. The first focuses on the attackers: Who were they? How are they regarded? How should their actions be characterized? How should they be sanctioned – if at all? The second set concerns the extent of Donald Trump's responsibility for what happened and how or whether he should be held accountable for his role in the events. A third set of questions focuses on reactions to the House committee's hearings and *Final Report*, including whether they had any effect on opinions surrounding January 6. To anticipate, I find they generally did not. Rather, the data show that, after the first few weeks following the attack, public opinion on most questions settled into stable configurations that strongly echoed the highly polarized reactions already provoked by Donald Trump and his stolen election lie. Contrary to some initial expectations, the invasion and trashing of the Capitol that Trump's lying inspired did little damage to his reputation among his erstwhile supporters, and he remains a serious candidate for reelection in 2024. Reactions to January 6 make it doubtful that even Trump's criminal trials – and, potentially, convictions – will have much effect on his support. I complete this section by considering the extent to which false beliefs about January 6 are sincerely held products of misinformation and motivated reasoning or exercises in partisan cheerleading and trolling.

1.2 Opinions of the Capitol Invaders

The invasion of the Capitol by a violent mob intent on preventing Congress's certification of Joe Biden's victory was a stunning, home-grown assault on American democracy. Most Americans were some combination of shocked, angry, appalled, or embarrassed by what they saw on news broadcasts of the event, and the opinions of the rioters were decisively negative, including those expressed by Republicans and Trump voters (Gramlich, 2022). Even Trump himself, who finally sent the Capitol invaders home on January 6 with "we love you. You're very special," felt compelled to denounce them the next day for having "defiled the seat of American democracy" and to vow they would pay for breaking the law.[2]

---

[1] The list of sponsors providing the surveys analyzed here is in the Appendix; they were accessed through the FiveThirtyEight website, the Roper Center archive, newspaper reports, and the survey's individual websites. The citations for each table list the sources according to the number assigned to them in the Appendix.

[2] From the transcript of a video recorded by Trump: "Like all Americans, I am outraged by the violence, lawlessness and mayhem.. ... America is, and must always be, a nation of law and order. The demonstrators who infiltrated the Capitol have defiled the seat of American democracy. To those who engage in the acts of violence and destruction: You do not represent our country, and to those who broke the law: You will pay" (quoted in Bump, 2021).

Responses to one of the first surveys on the event, the ABC News/*Washington Post* poll fielded January 10–13, 2021, show overwhelming popular condemnation of the rioters, with 80 percent strongly opposed to their actions (Table 1). However, reactions varied by party and presidential vote and especially by belief in Trump's stolen election lie (of which more in Section 1.7). In light of the rioters' stated motivation for storming the Capitol, it is not surprising that the respondents who denied that Biden won legitimately (32 percent in this survey) were much more likely to support the action, 20 percent compared to 2 percent of those who accepted Biden's legitimacy. Still, 60 percent of even the election-denying Trump voters opposed the action strongly. No wonder Trump felt obliged – very temporarily, it turned out – to condemn the invaders.

Other surveys taken during the two months after January 6 also found few people of any partisan persuasion offering favorable opinions of the rioters, with averages ranging from a low of 3 percent among Biden's voters to a high of only 16 percent among the most sympathetic subgroup, Trump's voters (Table 2).[3] In surveys taken over the next sixteen months, the overall proportion of favorable opinions nearly doubled, rising from five to eleven points depending on partisan category, with a maximum of about a quarter of Republicans and Trump voters viewing the Capitol invaders positively. The distribution of responses to this question was undisturbed by the House Select Committee's televised hearings or its final report delivered in December 2022.

1.3 Characterizations of the Capitol Invaders

Surveys reported far less consensus about how best to characterize the January 6 actors and their actions. In the December 2021 Ipsos poll, for example, 79 percent of Democrats and 89 percent of Biden voters viewed the invaders as criminals or right-wing domestic terrorists (Table 3). The comparable figures for Republicans and Trump voters were 27 and 23 percent, respectively, and they were much more likely to say the rioters were well-meaning but got carried away (23 and 28 percent, respectively) or were patriots fighting to preserve our freedoms. They were also much more inclined to characterize the rioters as left-wing or antifa (anti-fascist activists), a tendency especially pronounced among that majority of Trump voters (72 percent in this survey) who denied Biden's legitimacy. Republicans and Trump voters were also much more likely than Democrats or Biden voters to plead ignorance.

The idea that rioters were not Trump supporters but rather antifa or other leftists aiming to discredit Trump was floated by Trump himself on the day of

---

[3] The table combines responses to questions including favorable/unfavorable, approve/disapprove, and support/oppose as options.

Table 1 'Do you support or oppose the actions of people who stormed the United States Capitol last week to protest Biden's election as president?" (percent)

	All	Dem	Ind.	Rep.	Biden voters	Trump voters	Election deniers	Not deniers	Trump voters-deniers	Trump voters-Not deniers
Support strongly	5	1	5	10	0	10	13	1	14	1
Support somewhat	3	1	4	5	0	8	7	1	7	2
Oppose somewhat	9	3	12	12	2	13	16	4	13	14
Oppose strongly	80	95	77	67	97	64	58	93	60	80
No opinion	2	0	2	5	0	5	6	1	6	3

Source: ABC News/*Washington Post* Poll, January 10–13, 2021, Roper Center Dataset, https://doi.org/10.25940/ROPER–31118174.

Table 2 Favorable opinions of/support for/approval of rioters who breached the Capitol on January 6 (percent)

	All		Democrats		Independents		Republicans	
	Fav.	Unfav.	Fav.	Unfav.	Fav.	Unfav.	Fav.	Unfav.
January/February 2021 (9)	9	83	4	94	10	80	14	76
March 2021–May 2022 (12)	17	71	13	83	16	72	25	61
During hearings (7)	19	71	13	83	16	71	28	61
After hearings (16)	18	71	13	83	13	69	27	59

	Biden voters		Trump voters	
	Fav.	Unfav.	Fav.	Unfav.
January/February 2021 (6)	3	95	16	76
March 2021–May 2022 (9)	8	88	26	62
During hearings (5)	8	89	26	61
After hearings (10)	9	87	26	56

Note: The number of polls averaged is in parentheses.
Source: Survey sponsors 1, 8, 11, 15, 19, and 22 listed in the Appendix.

Table 3 Characterization of people who broke into the Capitol on January 6, 2021 (percent)

	All	Dem.	Ind.	Rep.	Biden voters	Trump voters	Election deniers	Not deniers	Trump voters-deniers	Trump voters-not deniers
They are criminals	34	39	40	23	42	21	19	45	12	35
They are right-wing domestic terrorists	22	40	20	4	47	2	2	35	1	4
They were well-meaning but got carried away in the moment	13	5	12	23	3	28	23	6	26	27
They are patriots who were fighting to preserve our freedoms	4	3	3	7	0	8	13	2	12	6
They are left-wing terrorists or antifa	6	1	4	15	1	16	22	1	30	1
Don't know	21	13	22	29	8	25	22	11	19	28

Source: Ipsos Poll December 3–7, 2021, Roper Center Dataset, https://doi.org/10.25940/ROPER–31119144.

Table 4 The Capitol rioters were predominantly Trump opponents/left-wing/antifa (percent)

	All	**Dem.**	**Ind.**	**Rep.**	**Biden voters**	**Trump voters**
Yes	37	19	35	61	15	72
No	44	66	51	19	72	12
Don't know	19	15	14	20	13	16

Note: The average for partisans is based on ten surveys (seven surveys for presidential voters) taken between January 2021 and July 2022.
Source: Survey sponsors 3, 11, 15, 24, and 31 listed in the Appendix.

the riot (H.R. Rep. No. 117–613, 2022: 84) and was initially endorsed by such right-wing luminaries as Rush Limbaugh and Fox News's Laura Ingram, Sean Hannity, and Tucker Carlson, as well as by some far-right members of Congress (Anderson, 2023). Carlson later claimed that the riot was not only provoked by leftists but also a trap sprung by the FBI to justify purging and jailing Trump supporters (McCarthy, 2021). The testimony of the rioters themselves, their past statements and affiliations, and the information brought out in judicial proceedings against them provide no support whatsoever for any such claims (Anderson, 2023; Pape, 2022a). That has not prevented their acceptance by majorities of Republicans and Trump voters and even a surprising number of Democrats (Table 4). On average in surveys asking whether those responsible were opponents rather than supporters of Trump, a little more than a third of respondents have said they were. It is the majority opinion among Republicans and Trump voters, but averages of 19 percent of Democrats and 15 percent of Biden voters also share it. The incidence of belief varies by education. For example, in the January 2021 American Perspectives Survey, 7 percent of Democratic college graduates said "antifa, the anti-facist activist group," was "mostly responsible for the violence that happened in the riots at the U.S. Capitol," compared to 22 percent of those who were not college graduates. Republicans also showed a strong education gradient, with 57 percent of non-college Republicans believing this allegation, compared to 37 percent of college graduates.[4] Thus consistent with the literature, at least some conspiratorial beliefs about January 6 were not confined to one party and were considerably more common among people with less education (Uscinski & Parent, 2014).

---

[4] Survey Center on American Life, American Perspectives Survey (January 21–30, 2021), www.americansurveycenter.org/download/jan-2021-american-perspectives-survey/.

The related notion that the incursion was a false-flag operation involving government agents as well as leftists receives less support, but a substantial proportion of Republicans and Trump voters responding to an Ipsos poll taken eleven months after the event said they believed it (Table 5). Even larger proportions professed ignorance, while less than a third recognized it as false. Only a tiny fraction (4 percent) of respondents who were not Republicans, Trump voters, or election deniers answered "true." Election deniers who voted for Trump were especially inclined to embrace this ancillary conspiracy theory, and most of its believers (69 percent overall, 88 percent among Trump voters) came from the ranks of election deniers.

It is no mystery why Trump supporters would want to shift the blame away from their own side and onto leftists or agents of the "deep state." Broadcast images of thugs attacking police and vandalizing the Capitol building would certainly be upsetting to people who think of themselves as patriotic Americans who deeply love their country. When far-right pundits and politicians offered dissonance-avoiding alternatives – blame the left and/or the feds – it was tempting to adopt them. It was, after all, the kind of perfidy to be expected from "radical left socialists" (Trump's habitual description of his Democratic opponents) and Trump's supposed deep-state antagonists, not from true patriots like themselves. It was also a question that invited partisan cheerleading (or more precisely, taunting) and disingenuous trolling of pollsters working for the mainstream news media, discussed more fully in Section 1.13.

A different question about the motivations of the Capitol invaders that allowed multiple responses was asked three times by the CBS News/ YouGov Poll between July 2021 and June 2022. Table 6 reports the average distribution of responses (there was little variation and no trend across these surveys). Respondents in all categories generally agreed that it was, among other things, a protest that went too far. Large majorities of Democrats and Biden voters and smaller majorities of independents also saw it as an attempt to nullify the election and keep Trump in power, an insurrection, an attempt to overthrow the government, or some combination of all three – by any description, a seditious assault on American democracy. These were decidedly minority views among Republicans and Trump voters, of whom 46–56 percent saw the rioters as defending freedom and/or acting out of patriotism. Be that as it may, the rioters were unquestionably "trying to overturn the election and keep Trump in power" – the whole point of their action was to "stop the steal" by blocking certification – so not checking off this option, which attracted only 36 percent of Republicans and 31 percent of Trump voters, required a clear denial of reality.

Table 5 True or false: "The people who broke into the United States Capitol on January 6th (2021) were actually undercover members of Antifa and government agents." (percent)

	All	Dem.	Ind.	Rep.	Biden voters	Trump voters	Election deniers	Not deniers	Trump voters– deniers	Trump voters-not deniers
True	12	4	9	23	3	26	35	4	45	4
False	55	72	60	31	79	31	20	75	18	57
Don't know	34	23	32	47	18	43	45	21	38	39

Source: Ipsos Poll, December 3–7, 2021, Roper Center Dataset, https://doi.org/10.25940/ROPER–31119144.

Table 6 "Thinking about the people who forced their way into the U.S. Capitol on January 6, 2021. Would you describe their actions as . . . " (Percent)

	All	**Dem.**	**Ind.**	**Rep.**	**Biden voters**	**Trump voters**
A protest that went too far	73	69	74	78	67	81
Trying to overturn the election and keep Trump in power	64	88	64	36	93	31
Insurrection	55	83	55	25	89	19
Trying to overthrow the U,S. government	55	84	55	20	83	14
Defending freedom	30	14	24	55	10	56
Patriotism	28	15	26	49	11	52

Note: Average of three CBS News/YouGov polls, July 14–17, 2021, December 17–20, 2021, June 22–24, 2022.

1.4 Legitimate Political Discourse?

Republican leaders eventually opted to whitewash or downplay the events of January 6 because the optics were so bad for their party. In February 2022, a resolution by the Republican National Committee censuring Republican representatives Liz Cheney and Adam Kinzinger for serving on the House committee appointed to investigate the riots charged that the committee was persecuting "ordinary citizens engaged in legitimate political discourse" (Dawsey & Sonmez, 2022). The Reploican National Committee (RNC) was quick to deny they meant those who had attacked the police or invaded and vandalized the Capitol, although these were the only "ordinary citizens" facing legal sanctions. Several surveys taken before and after the RNC's resolution had asked whether the action could be characterized as legitimate political discourse, with results listed in Table 7. Responding to the single poll asking the question immediately after the event, less than a quarter of respondents said the rioters were engaged in legitimate political discourse, but with a large partisan divide, 3 percent of Democrats compared to 47 percent of Republicans saying that they were. Support for the notion was a bit higher in later surveys, with a majority of Republicans opting for "legitimate discourse." Again, the House hearings had little evident effect on the distribution of opinion on this question. If anything, Democrats and Biden voters

Table 7 The people who broke into the Capitol were engaged in legitimate political discourse (percent)

	All		Democrats		Independents		Republicans	
	Yes	No	Yes	No	Yes	No	Yes	No
January 7, 2021 (1)	23	72	3	96	25	65	47	47
June 2021–March 2022 (4)	31	55	12	80	34	51	53	33
During hearings (4)	28	54	13	79	33	51	57	30
After hearings (5)	34	55	18	76	30	53	56	32

	Biden voters		Trump voters	
	Yes	No	Yes	No
June 2021–March 2022 (2)	6	87	65	20
During hearings (3)	8	86	63	21
After hearings (4)	14	82	63	24

Note: The number of surveys average is in parentheses.
Source: Survey sponsors 7, 11, 17, 22, and 27 listed in the Appendix.

grew more supportive of the idea, although this change is more likely to be random noise arising from the small number of surveys and house effects.

Finally, two surveys probed perceptions of the level of violence at the Capitol. Responding to the December 2021 AP-NORC survey, about two-thirds of the public said the events had been "extremely" or "very" violent, with the other third saying they were "somewhat," "not very," or "not at all" violent. Ninety percent of Democrats chose one of the first two options, compared to 55 percent of independents and 40 percent of Republicans.[5] A University of Maryland/*Washington Post* poll taken the same month found 54 percent saying those who entered the Capitol were "mostly violent," 19 percent "mostly peaceful," and the rest "equally violent and peaceful." Democrats split 78–5 on the first two options, independents, 55–18, Republicans, 26–36, Biden voters, 81–3, and Trump voters, 21–45. This survey also asked, "Do you think that some protesters injured police officers while trying to break into the U.S. Capitol on January 6, or did everyone act peacefully?" A large majority (87 percent) acknowledged the widely reported fact that the rioters had injured many police officers; it included 81 percent of Republicans, but 16 percent of them, and 23 percent of Trump voters, rejected that reality, another exercise in willful denial – or in trolling a pollster.[6]

1.5 Prosecute or Pardon the Invaders?

The partisan disparities in the characterization of the Capitol incursion and its perpetrators' motives are naturally echoed in opinions of how the rioters should be treated. In the three surveys taken shortly after the event, when disapproval of their behavior was at a peak (Table 2), very large majorities wanted the Capitol invaders to be prosecuted, including 84 percent of Republicans.[7] Since then, support for prosecution has waned, although a solid majority of Americans still support holding them legally accountable (Table 8). The falloff has been largest among Republicans, with support dropping sharply to about 40 percent by May 2021 and then remaining stable at this lower level thereafter. With hundreds of cases being settled by guilty pleas or convictions and hundreds more pending, Republicans and Trump voters have come to favor pardons for the guilty, which Trump has promised to do if he is returned to office in 2024 (Alfalo, 2022). Partisans are also far apart on their feelings about the sanctions meted out so far by the courts; 66 percent of Democrats and 70 percent of Biden voters in the 2022 ANES Pilot Study said they had been too mild, with only

---

[5] https://apnorc.org/wp-content/uploads/2022/01/Jan6-_topline.pdf.

[6] www.washingtonpost.com/context/dec-17-19-2021-washington-post-university-of-maryland-poll/2960c330-4bbd-4b3a-af9d-72de946d7281/.

[7] The presidential vote is not reported in these three surveys.

Table 8 People who broke into the Capitol should be: (percent)

	All		Democrats		Independents		Republicans	
	Yes	No	Yes	No	Yes	No	Yes	No
Prosecuted								
January–March 2021 (3)	89	9	99	1	88	10	84	15
May 2021–June 2023 (7)	60	24	84	10	55	26	40	41
Pardoned								
February 2022–January 2024 (6)	30	61	14	83	27	60	51	36

	Biden voters		Trump voters	
	Yes	No	Yes	No
Prosecuted				
May 2021–June 2023 (7)	91	6	34	47
Pardoned				
February 2022–June 2023 (4)	10	87	52	32

Note: The number of surveys averaged is in parentheses.
Source: Survey sponsors 8, 11, 19, 22, 23, and 26 listed in the Appendix.

10 percent of the former and 6 percent of the latter saying they were too harsh. Among Republicans and Trump voters, the breakdowns were 61 and 69 percent saying too harsh, and 13 and 9 percent saying too mild (American National Election Studies, 2022a).

Table 9 summarizes the data on public assessments of the Capitol invaders since January 6. Majorities of Americans have condemned the rioters, viewed them as insurrectionists rather than legitimate protesters, and said they should be prosecuted and not pardoned. Democrats and Biden voters are overwhelmingly of these opinions, with the largest but still a modest departure from consensus in the belief expressed by about one in five that antifa or other leftists contributed to the mayhem. Consensus is lower among Republicans and Trump voters. Nearly two-thirds view the invaders negatively, but nearly as many say they were engaged in legitimate political discourse. They are also divided on whether the invaders deserve prosecution or pardon. A curiosity here is that although 72 percent of Trump voters say the invaders were antifa, only a third want them prosecuted and more than half want them pardoned. I could not find the antifa question paired with questions about prosecution or pardon in any survey, so it remains uncertain how Trump's supporters reconcile these positions. This anomaly again suggests that, when available, the option of blaming the left for the riots is hard to resist among people otherwise inclined to excuse the rioters as patriotic defenders of freedom engaging in legitimate political discourse. The nature of these responses will be parsed in the discussion of partisan cheerleading in Section 1.13.

1.6 Trump's Responsibility

Donald Trump's responsibility for the Capitol invasion is in one sense indisputable: Had he accepted Biden's victory as legitimate and conceded as customary, it would never have happened. The invasion occurred only because the mob believed Trump's claim that he was the true winner and that the Democrats and Biden had stolen the election from him – and them.[8] Information in the House committee's *Final Report* makes it unlikely in the extreme that Trump was unaware or deluded enough to believe his own stolen election lies (although the claim that he really did believe them is central to his defense against the election interference indictments). Top officials in the departments of Justice and Homeland Security, senior White House staff, leaders of Trump's campaign management team, and Republican state election officials all told him repeatedly that no evidence could be found supporting allegations of consequential

---

[8] Some radical anti-government groups may also have used the event as an opportunity to pursue preexisting revolutionary aims, using Trump's lie as a rallying point and recruitment opportunity.

Table 9 Summary of opinions on the people who broke into the Capitol on January 6, 2021 (average percentages from surveys taken from January 2021 through September 2023)

	All	Dem.	Ind.	Rep.	Biden voters	Trump voters
Negative opinion of invaders (44, 30)	74	85	73	63	90	63
It was legitimate political discourse (14, 9)	31	14	32	55	10	63
It was an insurrection (17, 12)	53	79	51	27	86	21
Antifa/Trump opponents were to blame (11, 7)	37	20	35	61	19	72
They should be prosecuted (10, 6)	69	88	65	53	91	34
They should be pardoned (6, 4)	30	14	27	51	10	52

Note: The number of surveys averaged is in parentheses: left entry for partisans and right entry for presidential voters.
Source: Survey sponsors 1, 3, 7, 8, 11, 15, 17, 19, 22–24, 26, 27, and 31 listed in the Appendix.

fraud in any of the states he lost (H.R. Rep. No. 117–613, 2022: 202–230). Lacking such evidence, the more than sixty court challenges to state results mounted by his allies failed in all but one trivial case.[9] Trump nonetheless persisted in repeating the discredited allegations of fraud (as he does to this day), siding with a dubious cast of conspiracy promoters telling him what he – and a large majority of his MAGA followers – wanted to hear (H.R. Rep. No. 117–613, 2022: 22–27, 203–231).

Trump was also clearly responsible for summoning the protesters to Washington DC. He was the headliner at the January 6 rally organized by a coalition of pro-Trump groups aimed at preventing Congress from certifying Biden's victory, tweeting on December 19, "Big protest in D.C. on January 6th. Be there, will be wild!"[10] Speaking at the rally, held on the Ellipse south of the White House, Trump reiterated his stolen election lies, demanded Vice President Mike Pence use his (nonexistent) authority to block certification of the results, and encouraged his audience to march on the Capitol, telling them, "We have come to demand that Congress do the right thing and only count the electors who have been lawfully slated. . ... And we fight. We fight like hell. And if you don't fight like hell, you're not going to have a country anymore" (Associated Press, 2021). He promised and reportedly sought to head down to the Capitol with the crowd after the speech but could not overcome the Secret Service's strenuous objections (H.R. Rep. No. 117–613, 2022: 585–592).

Trump did not explicitly call on the crowd to use violence to "stop the steal" and at one point said, "I know that everyone here will soon be marching over to the Capitol building to peacefully and patriotically make your voices heard." But his speech was rife with violent imagery and calls to fight harder to prevent Biden's certification because he would be "an illegitimate president . . . and we can't let that happen" (Associated Press, 2021). Whether or not Trump deliberately encouraged his followers to use physical force to stop Congress from acting, most of the Capitol invaders thought they were doing his bidding. Trump watched the action unfolding on television and for more than three hours resisted entreaties from congressional allies, White House staff, right-wing media confidants, and his own family to tell the invaders to leave. Instead, about forty-five minutes into the invasion, he issued a tweet that further inflamed the rioters, berating Pence for not flouting federal law and the Constitution to keep him in office (H.R. Rep. No. 117–613, 2022: 596–597). Trump never ordered the National Guard, FBI, or any other federal law

---

[9] The one victory was in a case that stopped the counting of 270 votes in Pennsylvania (Danforth et al., 2022).

[10] Donald J. Trump: Tweets of December 19, 2020, The American Presidency Project, available at www.presidency.ucsb.edu/ documents/tweets-december-19-2020.

enforcement agency to assist DC and Capitol police in putting down the insurrection and by some accounts enjoyed what he was seeing (Costa, 2022; H.R. Rep. No. 117–613, 2022: 593–603).

In the aftermath, Republican congressional leaders Kevin McCarthy and Mitch McConnell explicitly blamed Trump for what they, their chambers, and a (largely) horrified country had just endured. Even when they declined to support his second impeachment, it was on the grounds that his presidency was over, not that he wasn't fully guilty as charged (Hulse & Fandos, 2021). And indeed, the notion that Trump bears little or no responsibility for the events of January 6 seems bizarrely perverse.[11] It has, nonetheless, a coherent logic if you accept Trump's claim of a stolen election. Although the claim is preposterous on its face and has been exhaustively debunked (Cassidy, 2022; Dale, 2022; Danforth et al., 2022; Grofman & Cervas, 2023; Jacobson, 2023b), large majorities of Republicans and Trump voters continue to believe it (Table 10).[12] During the weeks leading up to January 6, averages of 74 percent of Republicans and 82 percent of Trump voters endorsed the stolen election lie in one form or another, and from their ranks came the Capitol invaders (H.R. Rep. No. 117–613, 2022: 502–510). In the aftermath of the insurrection, support for the big lie fell by a few points, and it eroded a bit more after the House Select Committee's public hearings in the summer of 2022. But to this day, more than two-thirds of Republicans and 72 percent of Trump voters still accept it, and it remains a cornerstone of Trump's campaign to recapture the White House in 2024.

1.7 Election Denial

Because election denial was the root cause of the January 6 Capitol invasion and strongly influences beliefs and opinions about what happened and who is responsible, it merits a more detailed examination. Only tiny proportions of Democrats or Biden voters say the election was stolen, and virtually all of the independents who do so were Trump voters; so election denial is confined almost entirely to Trump supporters. Not all of them are deniers, however, and denial varies with demography, social environment, and political attitudes in revealing ways. Table 11 presents some illustrative data (for elaboration, see Jacobson, 2023b). Trump voters who are older, less educated, conservative, and white are more likely to deny Biden's legitimacy; perhaps surprisingly, so are women. Denial is also more prevalent where the social context is more supportive; it is more common the more rural and less urban the voter's community

---

[11] Trump's degree of blame for the violence is arguably more ambiguous (Lee, 2022).

[12] For specifics on question wording, see Jacobson (2023b: 133–166).

Table 10 Belief that Biden was not legitimately elected in 2020 (percent)

	All	Dem.	Ind.	Rep.	Biden voters	Trump voters
Election day to January 6, 2021 (23, 14)	36	5	35	73	3	82
January 7, 2021 to June 1, 2022 (115, 78)	35	5	35	71	3	77
During House hearings (12, 12)	37	8	38	70	4	72
After House hearings through January 2024 (88, 62)	35	7	37	67	3	72

Note: The number of surveys averaged is in parentheses: left entry for partisans and right entry for presidential voters.
Source: Survey organizations 1–3, 5, 8–12, 14–17, 19–24, and 26–28, 30, and 31 listed in the Appendix.

and the larger Trump's vote share in the voters' state. Combining these two contextual variables, belief in the election was stolen ranges from 57 percent among Trump voters living in urban areas in states Biden won decisively to 88 percent among those living in rural areas of states where Trump ran strongest. The incidence of denial among Trump voters also varies with their choice of "most watched" cable news network. The few who pick one of the two more liberal options, CNN or MSNBC, are much less likely to believe that Trump won. Belief among Fox News watchers is only slightly higher than among those who watch no cable news at all, about 80 percent. Fox had angered Trump supporters as well as Trump when its news staff stuck with their election-night call of a Biden victory, prompting some to migrate to rival right-wing networks, such as the One America News Network and Newsmax, which treated the official results more skeptically and provided platforms to big-lie promoters (Brooks, Lane and Reid, 2020; Paleologos, 2021).[13] These would fall into the "other cable" category, chosen by 11 percent of Trump voters, of whom 90 percent deny Biden's legitimacy.

Trump has regularly, with varying degrees of subtlety, given vent to racism, xenophobia, and sympathy for white supremacists (Montanaro, 2022; Scott, 2019; Sebastian, 2017; Serwer, 2018). Three entries derived from questions in the Nationscape survey (Tausanovich & Vavreck, 2020) measure the extent to

---

[13] Facing lawsuits, both networks eventually admitted they had no evidence of fraud.

Table 11 Expressed belief among Trump voters that Joe Biden was not the legitimate winner

Variable	%	Percent of Trump voters	Variable	%	Percent of Trump voters
All Trump voters	78	100	Racial resentment*		
Education			Low	55	32
Not college graduate	82	63	Middle	62	29
College graduate	72	37	High	77	39
Age			Relative discrimination*		
<30	62	9	More vs. Blacks	48	30
30–44	71	18	Same	67	44
45–64	81	41	More vs. whites	82	27
65+	83	32	Anti-immigrant scale*		
Gender			Low	48	20
Male	75	54	Middle	65	53
Female	81	46	High	79	27
Race			Opinion of Trump		
White	79	84	Very favorable	93	58
Non-white	73	16	Somewhat favorable	70	28
Ideology			Somewhat unfavorable	40	9
Liberal	45	4	Very unfavorable	29	5
Moderate	65	22			

Category		
Conservative	83	71
Type of community		
City	68	20
Suburb	77	39
Town	80	15
Rural	85	26
Trump state vote share		
<40%	68	16
40%–50%	78	36
50%–60%	80	37
>60	83	12
Most watched cable news		
CNN/MSNBC	39	6
None	78	46
Fox	80	37
Other cable	90	11
Opinion of Biden		
Very favorable	26	3
Somewhat favorable	22	4
Somewhat unfavorable	41	9
Very unfavorable	87	83
Opinion of Republican Party		
Very favorable	84	26
Somewhat favorable	78	44
Somewhat unfavorable	74	19
Very unfavorable	68	8
Opinion of Democratic Party		
Very favorable	29	2
Somewhat favorable	29	4
Somewhat unfavorable	54	10
Very unfavorable	85	81

Sources: *Economist*/YouGov Polls, January 2021–August 2022 (*N* = 34,972 Trump voters) except for the starred racial resentment, relative discrimination, and anti-immigrant scales, which are from the ten postelection waves of the Nationscape survey (*N* = 17,172 Trump voters)

which his voters share such sentiments: the standard racial resentment scale,[14] opinions on relative discrimination against Blacks and whites,[15] and a scale measuring anti-immigrant sentiment.[16] In all three cases, the more Trump's voters align with his illiberal attitudes, the more likely they are to say he won. The measure of white racial grievance – assessments of the relative levels of discrimination suffered by Blacks and whites – shows the strongest association. Of the 27 percent of Trump voters who say whites suffer more discrimination than Blacks, 82 percent said Trump won; among the small proportion at the extremes on these questions (claiming a great deal of discrimination against whites and none at all against Blacks), it is 94 percent.

Not surprising, election denial is most strongly related to opinions of Trump and Biden. Fifty-eight percent of Trump voters view him very favorably, and 87 percent of this segment deny Biden's legitimacy; 54 percent express a combination of a very favorable opinion of Trump and a very unfavorable opinion of Biden, and 96 percent of them deem Biden's election illegitimate. Opinions of the Democratic Party are also strongly related to the belief that Biden was not the legitimate winner; opinions of the Republican Party are less so, because even those with negative opinions the party are strongly inclined to endorse the big lie.

All of the variables in Table 11 are correlated with each other as well as with the belief that Biden was not legitimately elected, and in some cases causality may run in either direction. Trump voters especially hostile to Biden and his party may be more susceptible to the big lie, but believing the election was stolen may make them more hostile to Biden and Democrats; choice of news sources may reflect prior beliefs, but consuming them may also reinforce those beliefs. A full causal model is thus beyond what such data can support, but multivariate analyses of these data do identify the strongest associations, and the results confirm that predominant source of variation in Trump voters' beliefs

---

[14] The questions are "Generations of slavery and discrimination have created conditions that make it difficult for blacks to work their way out of the lower class" (5-point scale, strongly agree to strongly disagree) minus "Irish, Italian, Jewish, and many other minorities overcame prejudice and worked their way up. Blacks should do the same without any special favor" (same scale). The resulting scale ranges from −4 to 4; for this analysis, low is −4 to −2, middle is −1 to 1, and high is 2 to 4. The original source is Kinder and Sanders (1996).

[15] Constructed from two questions: "How much discriminations is there in the United States today against Blacks" (5-point scale, "a great deal" to "none at all") minus "How much discriminations is there in the United States today against whites" (same scale).

[16] Constructed from three options, "Deport all immigrants" (3-point scale, agree to disagree) minus "Create a path to citizenship for undocumented immigrants brought here as children (same scale) and minus "Create a path to citizenship for all undocumented immigrants" (same scale). The resulting scale ranges from −4 to 4; for this analysis, low is −3 to −2, middle is −1 to 1, and high is 2 to 3.

about Biden's legitimacy is their attitude toward Trump; the next strongest association is with white racial grievance (Jacobson, 2023b).

Commitment to Trump fuels election denial and, through it, has a powerful effect on how his supporters view what happened on January 6. Denying Biden's legitimacy has, among other things, freed large majorities of Trump voters to absolve him of blame for what happened despite his status as its *sine qua non*. The blame goes instead to the alleged election thieves: Biden, the Democrats, and their corrupt allies. From this perspective, in fighting to overturn the official results, Trump was, like the rioters in their own imaginations, fighting to preserve rather than subvert American democracy. Shortly after the riots, the ABC News/ *Washington Post* poll asked, "How much responsibility do you think (Donald) Trump bears for the (January 6, 2021) attack on the United States Capitol – a great deal, a good amount, just some or none at all?" The distribution of responses demonstrates how powerfully election denial shielded Trump from responsibility (Table 12). Among the 66 percent of respondents who deemed Biden's victory legitimate, 85 percent said Trump bore a great deal (69 percent) or a good amount (16 percent) of responsibility; only 4 percent said he had none at all. Among the 34 percent of respondents who denied Biden's legitimacy, 71 percent said Trump bore no responsibility at all; among Trump-voting election deniers (comprising 76 percent of all Trump voters), it was 74 percent. However, even the minority of Trump voters who were not election deniers declined to assign him much responsibility, with 64 percent saying "just some" or "none"; election denial was sufficient but not necessary for most of them to absolve Trump.

Later, during the House hearings, three Morning Consult polls asked how responsible various groups and individuals had been for the attack on the Capitol. Trump voters were more likely to hold Biden "very" or "somewhat" responsible (average, 43 percent) than Trump (26 percent), and Democrats in Congress (55 percent) than Republicans in Congress (22 percent).[17] Blaming Biden and the Democrats rather than Trump and the Republicans follows if you believe that the attack was provoked by Biden's election theft and the Democratic Congress's refusal to rectify it.

Additional surveys have asked a variety of questions gauging opinions on Trump's responsibility for the riots, with results summarized in Table 13.[18]

---

[17] Morning Consult polls, June 10–12, June 17–20, and July 8–10, 2022, https://morningconsult.com/ 2022/06/13/january-6-polling-prime-time-committee-hearing/; https://assets.morningconsult.com/ wp-uploads/2022/06/21132002/2206122_crosstabs_POLITICO_RVs_v1_6-22-22_SH.pdf; https://morningconsult.com/2022/07/12/jan-6-hearings-voters-trump-gop-standing/.

[18] Responses such as "very/somewhat," "a lot/some," "great deal/some," "great deal/good amount," "a great deal/quite a bit," "solely/mainly," "fully/partly," and "fully/largely" are classified as "yes"; responses such as "a little/none," "not much/none," "a little/not at all," and "not too/not at all" are classified as "no."

Table 12 Donald Trump's responsibility for the January 6 attacks (percent)

	All	Dem.	Ind.	Rep.	Biden voters	Trump voters	Election deniers	Not deniers	Trump voters-deniers	Trump voters-not deniers
Great deal	46	75	43	12	78	4	5	69	2	16
A good amount	12	14	12	9	14	7	3	16	3	21
Just some	14	4	17	22	4	24	19	9	20	36
None at all	28	6	27	56	2	64	71	4	74	28
No opinion	1	1	1	2	1	1	1	1	1	0

Source: ABC News/*Washington Post* Poll, January 10–13, 2021, Roper Center Dataset, https://doi.org/10.25940/ROPER–31118174.

Table 13 Is Trump responsible for the Capital invasion on January 6?
(percent)

	All		Democrats		Independents		Republicans	
	Yes	**No**	**Yes**	**No**	**Yes**	**No**	**Yes**	**No**
January–February 2021 (13)	59	34	91	7	58	34	25	69
March 2021–May 2022 (17)	55	39	88	9	52	40	22	73
During hearings (18)	55	38	86	10	52	39	24	70
After hearings (10)	53	37	83	12	51	33	22	70

	Biden voters		Trump voters	
	Yes	**No**	**Yes**	**No**
January/February 2021 (9)	92	5	22	72
March 2021–May 2022 (11)	91	6	13	82
During hearings (12)	90	7	18	73
After hearings (9)	89	7	16	77

Note: The number of surveys averaged is in parentheses.
Source: Survey sponsors 1, 5, 7, 9, 13, 16, 18, 19, 23, 24, 26, and 27 listed in the Appendix.

Most Americans assign Trump at least some substantial blame. The proportion doing so fell by a few points after February 2021 but thereafter remained stable, unchanged by the House hearings investigating the event, which had among other things highlighted Trump's culpability. Partisan differences are stark, with very large majorities of Democrats and Biden voters blaming Trump but less than a quarter of Republicans and Trump voters concurring.

The question of Trump's responsibility specifically for the violence produces a similar distribution but with slightly lower numbers, particularly among Republicans and Trump voters (Table 14). Again, the House hearings had little effect on opinions of Trump's culpability.

1.8 Sanctioning Trump?

The partisan divide is wider yet on the question of whether Trump should be sanctioned for his behavior leading up to and on January 6. The first option was a second impeachment. A week after the riot, the House voted 232–197 for an article of impeachment against Trump for "incitement of insurrection," with ten Republicans joining the unanimous Democrats. The Senate trial that followed ended on February 13 with Trump's second acquittal; the 57–43 vote for conviction (with seven Republicans and every Democrat voting to convict) fell ten votes short of the two-thirds required by the Constitution.

The public overall was more supportive of Trump's second impeachment than his first, averaging 52 percent for and 41 percent against (Table 15), compared to averages of 48 percent for and 46 percent against a year earlier. Support was one point higher among Democrats and three points higher among independents. The increase among Republicans was four points, up from 9 percent to 13 percent, leaving the partisan gap a couple of points smaller than for the first impeachment but still very wide at seventy-four points.[19] The gap between Biden and Trump voters was wider – eighty-two points. For congressional Republicans, holding Trump formally accountable meant defying a very large majority of their partisans, and most declined to do so no matter what they thought of Trump's culpability. Their prudence, if not courage, was confirmed when only two of the ten House Republicans who voted for impeachment returned to Congress after the 2022 election.

A similar distribution of opinion initially prevailed on the question of whether Trump deserved to be criminally prosecuted for the schemes to over-turn the election that culminated in the January 6 insurrection. Support for

---

[19] The averages for Trump's first impeachment are from twenty-six surveys taken in December 2019 and January 2020; for details, see Jacobson (2021a: 273–289). The differences between levels of support for the two impeachments are significant at $p < 0.01$ for all partisan categories (estimated with OLS regression with survey sponsor fixed effects).

Table 14 Did Trump incite the January 6 violence? (percent)

	All		Democrats		Independents		Republicans	
	Yes	**No**	**Yes**	**No**	**Yes**	**No**	**Yes**	**No**
January–February 2021 (7)	53	37	88	6	40	38	16	75
March 2021–May 2022 (3)	48	41	80	14	47	44	13	78
During hearings (3)	52	38	86	9	54	37	19	72
After hearings (5)	50	37	81	8	49	34	15	75

	Biden voters		Trump voters	
	Yes	**No**	**Yes**	**No**
January/February 2021 (4)	89	5	13	76
March 2021–May 2022 (2)	85	9	6	86
During hearings (2)	88	8	10	79
After hearings (4)	85	7	10	80

Note: The number of polls averaged is in parentheses.
Source: Survey sponsors 1, 3, 7, 9, 16, 22, 23, and 27 listed in the Appendix.

Table 15 Holding Trump accountable for January 6? (percent)

	All		Democrats		Independents		Republicans	
	Yes	No	Yes	No	Yes	No	Yes	No
He should be impeached (44)	52	41	87	9	49	43	13	83
He committed a crime/should be prosecuted								
January 2021–April2022 (4)	51	44	88	9	51	44	10	86
During hearings (14)	49	40	84	9	45	40	14	76
August 2022–July 2023 (21)	45	40	80	9	42	37	10	77
After indictments (20)	53	35	86	7	53	31	17	71

	Biden voters		Trump voters	
	Yes	No	Yes	No
He should be impeached (23)	91	6	9	87
He committed a crime/should be prosecuted				
January 2021–April 2022 (2)	92	6	6	91
During hearings (9)	89	5	9	82
August 2022–July 2023 (15)	84	7	7	84
After indictments (9)	91	4	10	79

Note: The number of polls averaged is in parentheses.
Source: Survey sponsors 1, 2, 5–7, 9, 12, 13, 15, 16, 18, 19, 20, 23, 24, and 27 listed in the Appendix.

prosecution was highest among Democrats and independents in the three months after the event, but it fell off in surveys taken during and after the hearings until his August 2023 indictments, after which it surpassed its pre-hearings level, albeit slightly. Post-indictment, opposition to prosecution fell as much as support rose, leaving net support at eighteen points, up from an average of five points during the previous year. Republicans' support for prosecution rose a few points higher after the indictment but remained very low at 17 percent.[20] Although in all but two of the sixty surveys I have found that asked the question, at least a plurality has favored prosecuting Trump, and stark partisan differences guarantee that the court action will be highly divisive.

Of course, people who do not hold Trump responsible for the incursion would not want him prosecuted for it. In the January 2021 ABC News/*Washington Post* survey, for example, support for charging Trump with a crime split as expected: those who thought he bore a "great deal" of responsibility broke 90–9 in favor of charging him, a "good amount," 70–24, "just some," 22–70, and "none at all," 6–92 (who were this 6 percent?). Opposition to criminal charges in this poll was linked to presidential preference and election denial even more strongly than to assignment of responsibility (Table 16). Only 4 percent of election deniers, 1 percent of them among Trump voters, favored bringing charges.[21] The prevalence of belief in Trump's big lie among his partisans and voters clearly precludes any bipartisan effort to hold him accountable, but even the minority of his supporters who accepted Biden's legitimacy were overwhelmingly opposed to prosecution even in the immediate aftermath of the riots.

Table 17 summarizes the data on opinions of Trump's complicity in the events of January 6 and whether he should be held accountable. The partisan differences are even wider than for those regarding the Capital invaders (Table 9). Democrats and Biden voters are decisively of the opinion that he was responsible for the violence and ought to be held accountable for it. Republicans and Trump voters are much less likely to blame him and even less likely to want him punished.

1.9 Support for Investigating the January 6 Capitol Invasion

The Trump administration's violent coda on January 6 was, among other things, an acute embarrassment to the Republican Party. Its congressional leaders initially condemned the incursion and blamed Trump for provoking it, but when large majorities of their partisans stuck with Trump, they quickly

---

[20] I will have more to say about reactions to these and Trump's other indictments in Section 2.

[21] Similarly, when asked, in the January 10–13 NPR/Marist Poll, "Do you think Congress should or should not continue to take action against President (Donald) Trump for the events at the United States Capitol (the January 6, 2021 storming of the Capitol) after he leaves office?" only 4 percent of election deniers said Congress should take action, compared with 72 percent of non-deniers.

Table 16 "As you may know, (Donald) Trump encouraged his supporters to march to the United States Capitol, where a riot followed (January 6, 2021). Do you think Trump should be charged with the crime of inciting a riot, or do you think he should not be charged?"

(percent)

	All	Dem.	Ind.	Rep.	Biden voters	Trump voters	Election deniers	Not deniers	Trump voters-deniers	Trump voters-not deniers
Should be charged	54	90	54	12	93	5	4	82	1	12
Should not be charged	43	9	42	84	5	92	95	14	98	73
No opinion	3	1	4	4	3	2	1	3	1	6

Source: ABC News/*Washington Post* Poll, January 10–13, 2021, Roper Center Dataset, https://doi.org/10.25940/ROPER–31118174.

Table 17 Summary of opinions regarding Donald Trump and the Capitol invasion on January 6, 2021 (average percentages from surveys taken from November 2020 through November 2023)

	All	Dem.	Ind.	Rep.	Biden voters	Trump voters
Election was stolen from Trump (215, 154)	36	6	36	70	3	75
Trump is responsible for incursion (52, 36)	55	87	53	23	90	17
Trump provoked violence (17, 12)	51	85	50	15	87	9
Trump should be impeached (43, 23)	52	87	49	13	91	9
Trump committed a crime/ should be prosecuted/ support indictment (61, 35)	49	84	47	14	87	9

Note: The number of surveys averaged is in parentheses – left entry for partisans and right entry for presidential voters.
Source: Survey sponsor 1–3, 5–10, 12–16, and 18–27 listed in the Appendix.

reconsidered, apparently deciding that their best strategy was to put the whole thing behind them as swiftly as possible. When that proved impossible – Trump's continuing rants about having the election stolen from him didn't help, nor did the ongoing judicial proceedings against the rioters – some sought to rewrite history along the lines promoted by Trump and some of his allies in Congress and the right-wing media, downplaying the ugliness and violence and recasting the invaders as "ordinary tourists," "legitimate protesters," or America-loving patriots (Itkowitz, 2021). But even the majority of congressional Republicans who were not revisionists did not welcome an investigation that would remind Americans of what they had witnessed on January 6.

In May 2021, a proposal to set up an evenly balanced bipartisan commission, modeled on the 9/11 commission, to investigate the January 6 events passed the House with support from thirty-five Republicans as well as every Democrat but fell to a Senate filibuster when minority leader McConnell opted to oppose it. The House (all Democrats and two Republicans) then passed a resolution on June 30, 2021, entitled (and effectively) "Establishing the Select Committee to

Investigate the January 6th Attack on the United States Capitol," with eight members to be appointed by House speaker Nancy Pelosi and five by minority leader McCarthy "in consultation" with the speaker. Two of McCarthy's proposed appointees, Jim Banks and Jim Jordan, had actively sought to overturn the 2020 results (Itkowitz, 2021).[22] When Pelosi vetoed them, McCarthy refused to appoint replacements or to participate any further in the process. Pelosi then appointed two Republicans herself, Cheney and Kinzinger, the only sitting House Republicans who had voted to establish the committee and for the post-riot impeachment resolution.

The committee held ten televised hearings during 2022, eight of them in June and July. It issued a comprehensive report on December 22 that spelled out in great detail what had happened and who had been involved. It documented Trump's various unlawful schemes to overturn the election results, his role in provoking the rioters, his failure to deploy any federal law enforcement agency to deal with the ensuing violence, and his refusal to ask the rioters to leave the Capitol for more than three hours after they had first stormed in. The most damning testimony came from Republicans who had worked in Trump's administration or on his campaign, which did not prevent his supporters in Congress and the media from joining him in denouncing the hearings as a partisan witch hunt. This became the orthodox view of Republican identifiers and Trump voters, with averages of 76 percent of the former and 83 percent of the latter expressing it in the three surveys that posed the question during or after the hearings (the respective averages for Democrats and Biden voters were 9 percent and 6 percent).[23]

Public support for the committee reiterated the familiar partisan divide. Support for some kind of investigation was highest in 2021, with about two-thirds favoring it, including 90 percent of Democrats and a third of Republicans (Table 18). The actual House committee drew less but still majority backing, with little difference between opinions registered before, during, or after its hearings. The subsets of Biden and Trump voters were a few points less enamored with the committee after the public hearings. It may have made a difference in how the question was worded; more people said they "supported" the committee than "approved" of it, perhaps reflecting some disappointment at what it was able to accomplish. But this may also be a survey house effect, as the *Economist*/YouGov survey accounts for all

---

[22] Both had joined the failed suit to have the Supreme Court throw out the results in four states and had voted on January 6 against certifying the results from Arizona and Pennsylvania.

[23] *Economist*/YouGov polls, June 11–14 and June 18–21, 2022, at https://today.yougov.com/topics/politics/explore/topic/The_Economist_YouGov_polls?content=survey; NPR/Marist Poll, March 20–23, 2023, at https://maristpoll.marist.edu/polls/biden-the-issues-facing-the-nation/.

Table 18 Opinions on US House Select Committee hearings on Capitol invasion (percent)

	All		Democrats		Independents		Republicans	
	Pos.	Neg.	Pos.	Neg.	Pos.	Neg.	Pos.	Neg.
Hearings in general								
August–December 2021 (3)	65	31	90	8	64	32	35	61
Select Committee								
Before public hearings (3)	51	33	78	10	48	34	25	61
During public hearings (10)	51	35	80	10	44	37	23	64
After public hearings (10)	51	36	79	13	43	34	23	65
"Support" question (11)	60	32	87	9	55	32	31	58
"Approve" question (15)	46	37	76	12	40	38	20	67

	Biden voters		Trump voters	
	Pos.	Neg.	Pos.	Neg.
Select Committee				
Before hearings (3)	83	7	20	68
During public hearings (8)	84	8	15	75
After public hearings (5)	77	12	9	81
"Support" question (2)	83	7	21	67
"Approve" question (14)	81	9	13	77

Note: The number of polls averaged is in parentheses.

Source: Survey sponsors 5, 9, 16, 17, 21, and 23 listed in the Appendix.

but one of those using the "approve" question. Still, the unmistakable message is that the opinions of the committee were highly partisan and quite stable throughout the process.

1.10 Were the Hearings Consequential?

Data presented in the previous sections suggested that the House hearings had little effect on the aggregate opinion of Capitol invaders or Donald Trump's responsibility for their actions. Several surveys asked people directly whether the hearings affected their opinions, and the results confirm that they reinforced much more than they altered existing beliefs. Of course, to be influenced, people had to pay at least some attention to the hearings. In nine surveys taken between June 22 and November 17, 2022, that asked the question, an average of 22 percent of Americans said they followed them "very closely" or paid "a lot" of attention to them and an average of 28 percent said they ignored them entirely. About half fell into the middle categories, paying at least some attention (variously measured by the questions), and that proportion held for every partisan subgroup. But Democrats were much more likely to be in the most than in the least attentive category, 39 percent to 13 percent, while among Republicans the proportions were almost exactly reversed, 12 percent to 40 percent.[24] Democrats were also more likely to say the hearings changed their mind about what had happened (Table 19, Question 1), but the maximum reached only 15 percent after the last substantive hearing in October. The proportion of Republicans who said the hearings changed their mind was no greater than 5 percent in any survey and was down to 3 percent in the October survey.

Direct survey questions about whether new information or events have changed a respondent's mind probably underestimate the frequency of opinion change (Graham & Coppock, 2021). Asked a different way – how the hearings affected people's opinions of the seriousness of the January 6 incursion and of Trump's level of involvement in it – the July Suffolk University/*USA Today* Poll found a considerably larger share of respondents reporting some opinion change, although it was mainly in the direction of their partisan leanings (Question 2). Overall, about 40 percent of respondents reported changing their opinions, with about 80 percent of this subset saying that the events were more serious and that Trump was more involved than they had thought. But Democrats and Republicans gave sharply different responses to both questions, with solid majorities of Democrats opting for "more" and almost none for "less," and two-thirds of the small share of Republicans who reported changed opinions opting for "less."[25]

---

[24] Survey sources 9, 17, 22, 24, 26, and 27 listed in the Appendix.
[25] Suffolk University/*USA Today* poll, July 22–25, 2022, www.suffolk.edu/academics/research-at-suffolk/political-research-center/polls/national/2022.

Table 19 The reported effects of the House Select Committee Hearings (percent)

1. "Have the recent House January 6 Committee hearings changed your mind about what happened at the Capitol that day or who is responsible, or have the hearings not changed your mind?"[a]

	All		Democrats		Independents		Republicans	
	Yes	No	Yes	No	Yes	No	Yes	No
June 24–27, 2022	6	90	7	90	6	89	5	91
July 28–August 1, 2022	8	89	10	89	8	88	5	92
October 13–17, 2022	8	86	15	81	8	86	3	83

2. "How have the hearings changed your opinion about what happened on Jan. 6/about then-president Donald Trump's role in the Jan. 6 attack?"[b]

	Seriousness of January 6				Extent of Trump's involvement			
	All	Dem.	Ind.	Rep.	All	Dem.	Ind.	Rep.
More	32	56	31	7	32	59	29	6
Less	7	2	4	15	8	1	5	17
Opinion unchanged	56	39	59	69	56	38	60	69

3. "Has the House Select Committee on January 6th presented convincing evidence that Donald Trump sought to prevent or delay certification of the results of the 2020 presidential election or has the evidence not been convincing?"[c]

	All		Democrats		Independents		Republicans	
	Yes	No	Yes	No	Yes	No	Yes	No
July 5–12, 2022	52	48	84	15	42	58	18	82
September 7–14, 2022	52	48	83	17	46	53	20	80

[a] Monmouth University Polling Institute, www.monmouth.edu/polling-institute/reports/.

[b] Suffolk University/*USA Today* Poll, July 22–25, 2022, www.suffolk.edu/academics/research-at-suffolk/political-research-center/polls/national/2022.

[c] Marquette University Supreme Court Poll, https://law.marquette.edu/poll/category/results-and-data.

Responses to the third question in Table 19 testify to the power of partisan priors in shaping responses to any question concerning Trump. This question asked if the hearings had produced "convincing evidence that Donald Trump sought to prevent or delay certification of the results."[26] Nearly half the respondents said no. This is astonishing on its face, for the whole, openly stated aim of Trump's January 6 rally was to persuade Congress and/or Mike Pence to do precisely that. In his speech at the rally, Trump put it this way: "States want to revote. The states got defrauded. They were given false information. They voted on it. Now they want to recertify. They want it back. All Vice President Pence has to do is send it back to the states to recertify and we become president and you are the happiest people" (Naylor, 2021). While Trump was speaking, his campaign highlighted the fight to halt certification in a fundraising email.[27] Later, while the rioters were inside the Capitol, Trump tweeted, "Mike Pence didn't have the courage to do what should have been done to protect our Country and our Constitution, giving States a chance to certify a corrected set of facts, not the fraudulent or inaccurate ones which they were asked to previously certify. USA demands the truth!" (H.R. Rep. No. 117–613, 2022: 596). This was on top of Trump's widely reported earlier efforts to prevent or repeal certification of the vote in swing states, now subject to the DC and Georgia indictments. That 80 percent of Republicans say they were not convinced, even by the evidence of Trump's own words, that he wanted to block certification of the results is remarkable. Not paying attention is an insufficient explanation; their responses point to a practiced habit of rejecting any account of events that might reflect badly on Trump no matter how well founded it might be. The committee hearings and *Final Report* could not penetrate this mindset.

This does not mean the House hearings were inconsequential. They failed to move the needle on aggregate opinions of Trump and the Capitol invaders, but they did remind people already inclined to view them critically of the gravity of the attack and Trump's prominent role in it. More importantly, the investigations, testimony, and carefully detailed *Final Report* provided the impetus and initial evidence for the indictments of Trump and his confederates a year later.

---

[26] Marquette Law School Supreme Court polls, https://law.marquette.edu/poll/category/results-and-data/.

[27] "TODAY will be a historic day in our Nation's history. Congress will either certify, or object to, the Election results. Every single Patriot from across the Country must step up RIGHT NOW if we're going to successfully DEFEND the integrity of this Election" (H.R. Rep. No. 117–613, 2022: 788).

1.11 Expressive Responding, Partisan Cheerleading, and Trolling

Responses to politically charged factual questions, like many examined here, raise the issue of sincerity. Do respondents who get it wrong really believe what they say, or do they just take the position that supports their side without actually believing it, creating the large observed partisan gaps in beliefs about reality? Evidence that "expressive responding" or "partisan cheerleading" can exaggerate the prevalence of false beliefs has been reported in several studies (e.g., Bullock et al., 2015; Schaffner & Luks, 2018; Ross & Levy, 2023). Another source of distortion could be the disingenuous trolling of rival partisans and/or pollsters working for the mainstream news media (Lopez & Hillygus, 2018). A review of twelve recent studies found only limited evidence for insincere responding in most contexts, however; it was detectable in some but usually accounted for only a modest portion of the partisan gap in responses to divisive factual questions (Malka & Adelman, 2022).

1.12 Is Belief in the Big Lie Sincere?

Responses to some factual questions regarding January 6 are certainly open to suspicions of insincerity: Do most Republicans and Trump voters really believe that the election was stolen, that antifa and government agents were mostly responsible for the Capitol incursion, and that Trump was not trying to prevent or delay certification of the election results? Or are they just expressing solidarity with Trump and their party or contempt for liberals and mainstream media? The answer matters most for the stolen election question because the denial of Biden's legitimacy is so strongly associated with a range of other opinions regarding January 6. Three studies, using separate methodologies, have concluded that expressed beliefs that the election was stolen are indeed genuine (Cuthbert & Theodoridis, 2022; Fahey, 2022; Graham & Yair, 2023). This conclusion is reinforced by the results of a panel study that asked about confidence in the 2020 election results in three waves taken in 2020, 2021, and 2022. The study found responses to be highly stable across waves, "similar to those for demographic variables or long-term stable identities such as partisanship" (Levendusky et al., 2023: 11).[28]

---

[28] The question asks if the respondent is not at all, not too, somewhat, or very confident that the "2020 election was conducted fairly and accurately." On average over all three waves, 47 percent of Trump voters are not at all confident and 32 percent, not too confident. The reliability coefficient for responses to this question is 0.93, with between-wave stability estimates of between 0.90 and 0.95 (Levendusky et al., 2023). A study using rolling cross sections between October 27, 2022 and January 29, 2023 ($N = 20,000$) also reported no temporal decline in belief in the big lie (Arseneaux & Truex, 2023).

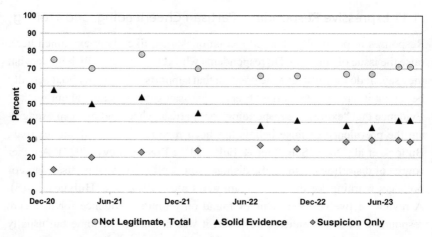

Figure 1 "Do you think that Joe Biden legitimately won enough votes to win the presidency, or not?) (If No, ask:) Do you think there's been solid evidence of that, or is that your suspicion only?"

This is not to say these beliefs are held with great or enduring confidence, however. Since January 2021, the CNN poll has asked nine times whether "Joe Biden legitimately won enough votes to win the presidency, or not?" For those answering no, the follow-up was "Do you think there's been solid evidence of that, or is that your suspicion only?" Figure 1 displays the trends in Republican responses. The proportion denying Biden's legitimacy has fallen from 75 percent in the first poll to 70 percent in the two most recent surveys, close to the average decline reported in Table 10. But the proportion saying "solid evidence" has fallen more steeply, from 58 to 40 percent, while the proportion saying "suspicion only" has risen from 13 to about 30 percent.

The absence of "solid evidence" has thus become somewhat more widely acknowledged by Republicans. Nonetheless, the belief that the election was stolen from Trump remains widespread because it has never depended on evidence. Anti-Trump Republican strategist Sarah Longwell, reporting on her conversations with a focus group of believers, observed that "For many of Trump's voters, the belief that the election was stolen is not a fully formed thought. It's more of an attitude, or a tribal pose. They know something nefarious occurred but can't easily explain how or why" (Longwell, 2022). A believer in Wisconsin, confronted by an NPR reporter with evidence that the election was legitimate, responded, "with broad-brush pronouncements such as 'they found emails,' and vague, baseless references to ballot harvesting, big money and the 'deep state.' He [said] nothing will ever convince him the election wasn't stolen. . . . 'We all know the whole game is rigged'" (Smith, 2022). Another Trump supporter, a co-founder of the Georgia Tea Party movement, told a reporter that she was sure voter fraud was widespread even if she could offer no specific examples: "You can't see God, but you know he is there" (Jarvie, 2020).

Believers' inability to reference specific, confirmed accounts of consequential fraud (none being available) helps to explain why so few of the tens of millions of Americans who said the presidential election had been stolen from Trump (and them) joined public protests, peaceful or otherwise, after the election – a fact that has misled some observers into concluding that most of them don't really believe the election was stolen (Musa al-Gharbi, quoted in Edsall (2023). Vague and diffuse notions about how, where, and by whom the "big steal" was carried off, along with the piecemeal, decentralized process of counting, recounting, and litigating votes, denied believers a specific target for outrage and a focal point for coordinating mass protests. Congress served this need poorly. Its involvement came at the end of the process and was essentially ceremonial; its members and Pence could be faulted only for failing to find some excuse for rejecting multiple official state results despite the lack of any concrete factual or constitutional basis for doing so. Goaded by Trump, the Capitol invaders did fault them, but most election deniers could not bring themselves to support their project; rejection of Biden's legitimacy was nearly three times as common as an endorsement of an action aimed at preventing his "illegitimate" certification.[29] A thought experiment: Suppose Congress or Pence had nullified state results and tried to hand the presidency to Trump. It is unimaginable that protests by Democrats and Biden supporters would not have been orders of magnitude larger, more widespread, and more sustained than what was observed in Washington DC on January 6, because the protesters would have had no doubt whatsoever about who stole the election and where and how they did it.[30]

1.13 Are Beliefs about the Capitol Invaders Sincere?

While election denial was apparently sincere if unfocused, blaming antifa or the deep state for the mayhem is a strong candidate for partisan cheerleading.

---

[29] For example, in three Yahoo News/YouGov polls that asked both questions, an average of 63 percent of Republicans and 67 percent of Trump voters said "the election was rigged and stolen from Trump," but only 23 percent of the former and 24 percent of the latter said "the January 6 attack on the U.S. Capitol was justified." Yahoo News/YouGov polls, May 24–26, 2021 and June 10–13 and June 24–27, 2022. Compare also the relevant entries for Republicans and Trump voters in Tables 9 and 10.

[30] Told to expect an explosion of protests if they prevailed, Jeffrey Clark, one of Trump's indicted co-conspirators in the scheme to overturn the election, is said to have replied, "Well, that's why there's an Insurrection Act" – that is, whatever protests overturning the election provoked could be put down by military force (Stanley-Becker, 2023).

Table 20 "How much are each of the following to blame for the January 6 attack on the Capitol?" (responses of Trump voters, percent)

	A great deal/some blame	Most blame
Donald Trump	21	5
Republicans who claimed the election had been stolen	36	4
Trump supporters who gathered at the US Capitol	39	7
Left-wing protesters trying to make Trump look bad	82	55
Right-wing groups like the Proud Boys	45	13

Source: Yahoo News/YouGov Poll, June 24–27, 2022 at https://docs.cdn.yougov.com/g0hxil9opn/20220624_yahoo_tabs.pdf.

People who genuinely believe January 6 was a false-flag operation initiated by the left would be unlikely to take the positions expressed by Trump supporters on other questions regarding the Capitol attackers. Consider the data in Table 9. Although an average of 72 percent of Trump voters say the invaders were mainly antifa, only a third want them prosecuted and more than half want them pardoned. If the violent thugs were Trump's leftist enemies in disguise, why the reluctance to prosecute and readiness to pardon them? Why not take the punitive attitude of Biden voters who think the invaders were right-wing insurgents – 91 percent favoring prosecution? It is also extremely doubtful that the majority of Trump voters who said the invaders were patriots, defenders of freedom, or engaged in legitimate protest (Tables 6 and 7) had antifa in mind.

The actual pattern of responses suggests that most Republicans and Trump voters share the common view that the Capitol invaders were Trump supporters protesting and trying to "stop the steal" and, as such, consider them deserving of some sympathy if not admiration. But when surveys offer the option of blaming the left, Trump voters were eager to seize it even if they also found it hard to deny that some on their side were also involved. In the June 24–27, 2022, Yahoo News/YouGov poll, for example, 82 percent of Trump voters said left-wing protesters bore a great deal or some blame for the attack, while 45 percent said the same of right-wing groups and 39 percent said it of Trump supporters (Table 20). Some thus faulted both sides, but when asked to assign the most blame, the consensus choice was the left, and only a tiny fraction named Trump. However spurious the false-flag claim, questions referencing it gave Trump supporters an opportunity for partisan cheerleading, inviting them to redirect criticism from their own side to their enemies, and most accepted it.

An even clearer instance of "expressive responding" is the 80 percent of Republicans who said they were not convinced that Trump wanted to block certification of the results on January 6. Trump could not have been more explicit about this demand, the focus of his January 6 speech urging the march on the Capitol; two years later, he was still insisting that Pence should have acted (Fortinsky, 2022). Some Republicans may have missed Trump's call to block Biden's certification by tuning out the news of January 6 and the later House investigation, but it strains credulity to think that so many remained so oblivious. A more plausible interpretation is that by denying a description of Trump's behavior on January 6 that might put him in a bad light, they were expressing solidarity with him and contempt for his critics.

The same would apply to the approximately two-thirds of Republicans and Trump voters who denied that the attackers were "trying to overturn the election and keep Trump in power" although it was their explicitly stated goal; most Republicans refused to attribute arguably seditious motives to people on their side. On a smaller scale, it is most unlikely that many of the 16 percent of Republicans and 23 percent of Trump voters who said that no police officers were injured on January 6 genuinely believed it. The exceptions might be the few sufficiently addled to buy the claim that the whole thing had been staged – a notion circulated in a meme Trump "re-truthed" on his Truth Social platform in the summer of 2023: "January 6 will go down in history as the day the government staged a riot to cover up the fact that they certified a fraudulent election" (Rissman, 2023). The rest could only be trolling Trump's detractors and mainstream pollsters.

1.14 Motivated Reasoning

Although answers to some questions about January 6 and its participants probably represent expressive responding or trolling pollsters, the broader and more consistent source of misinformed responses is motivated reasoning (Kunda, 1990; Lodge & Tabor, 2013). People tend to absorb and evaluate information that touches on their current attitudes and beliefs – especially those that are strongly held and linked to their sense of self – in ways that reinforce rather than erode them. Accuracy is not necessarily a priority: "In motivated reasoning, . . . it is important not just to get the right outcome, but also a certain preferred outcome, regardless of correctness." (Lebo & Cassino, 2007). Getting the preferred outcome is facilitated by:

- Selective exposure: paying attention to information sources likely to confirm prior opinions and beliefs and avoiding or ignoring sources likely to challenge them. As discussed in Section 2, there was no shortage of pundits and politicians circulating the big lie and the antifa canard. The strong association between election denial and cable news preference displayed earlier in Table 11 points to selective exposure, as is the relatively small share of Republicans who paid a lot of attention to the House hearings.
- Selective perception: perceiving new information accurately when it is consistent with prior beliefs and misperceiving it when it is not.
- Selective memory: remembering things consistent with prior beliefs and attitudes and forgetting or misremembering things that are inconsistent with them.
- Motivated skepticism and confirmation bias: putting time and cognitive effort into picking apart arguments or questioning information that challenges current opinions, while accepting uncritically information that appears to confirm them.

Everyone is subject to the cognitive biases induced by motivated reasoning in defense of strongly held attitudes and beliefs. Commitment to a political party or leader often creates potent incentives to engage in it, evidenced here by the wide partisan opinion gaps appearing repeatedly in response to questions about January 6. Popular perceptions of and reactions to events of that day and those involved were also strongly refracted through attitudes toward Donald Trump, an extraordinarily polarizing figure. They also reflected a fractured information environment that offered anyone in the market reasons to downplay or dismiss the events of January 6 as of minor importance and irrelevant to their opinions of Trump and his party.

2 Explanations and Implications

2.1 Introduction

The storming of the Capitol by a violent mob bent on stopping certification of Joe Biden's victory initially shocked and appalled Americans across the political spectrum. It showed what extreme partisan zeal, inflamed by an angry loser unable to admit the truth, could lead to. It challenged Trump's supporters to reconsider their allegiance to him and his stolen election lie. And it forced Republican politicians to weigh devotion to their party and careers against devotion to the institutions of American democracy. For a brief moment, it seemed that Trump's grip on his supporters and consequent hold on Republican elites in Congress and elsewhere would be significantly degraded. In the end, however, the events of January 6 inflicted only limited damage on Trump's standing among his erstwhile supporters, thus dissuading most Republican leaders from openly breaking with him, explicitly rejecting his big lie, and holding him accountable for its consequences. Elite and popular reactions to January 6 thus embodied and reinforced, rather than tempered, partisan polarization across the American political system.

2.2 Effects of January 6 on Republicans' Opinions of Trump

Trump's favorability ratings among Republicans did suffer a modest decline after January 6, falling from an average of 86 percent favorable in polls between the election and the riots to an average of 82 percent in the three months afterward. From April 2021 until just before the hearings in June 2022, it averaged 81 percent and from then through the November midterm, 80 percent. After the 2022 midterm and through Trump's first indictment in April 2023, the average fell to 75 percent;[31] the Republicans' weaker-than-expected midterm showing arguably did as much to tarnish Trump's image among ordinary Republicans as had the assault on the Capitol (Jacobson, 2023a). Recall from Table 10 that Republicans' belief in the big lie also fell similarly, from 74 percent prior to January 6 to 71 percent in the months afterward and eventually to 67 percent. Despite some modest attrition, then, Trump's standing with Republican voters and their belief in his stolen election lie has remained very high. As of the end of 2023, Trump was running far ahead of every potential Republican challenger for the 2024 nomination and was the odds-on favorite to head the Republican ticket for a third time.[32] His four criminal indictments on a total of ninety-one felony charges have yet to alter this status and may have even strengthened it; his favorability rating among Republicans edged back up to 79 percent over the eight months following his first indictment in April 2023.

The limited impact of January 6 on Trump's support reiterates a pattern persisting since his first presidential campaign. Trump's actions and their consequences have repeatedly raised questions about his fitness to serve as president: his bragging about sexually assaulting women, his obstructing the Mueller investigation, his calling racist demonstrators "fine people," his attempt to extort Ukraine to go after Biden, and his inept and lethal handling of the COVID-19 pandemic. Added to the list more recently are his loss of a civil suit for sexually abusing and defaming a department store saleswoman and his four

---

[31] Averages from 388 polls from survey sponsors 2, 3, 5, 7, 8, 10, 16, 17, 19, 22–24, and 27 listed in the Appendix.

[32] Trump held an average lead of nearly fifty points over his closest rival, Ron DeSantis, in polls taken in November 2023; see www.realclearpolitics.com/epolls/2024/president/us/2024_repub lican_presidential_nomination-7548.html.

indictments for falsifying business records to cover up hush money payments to a porn-star paramour, hiding classified documents at Mar-a-Lago, and conspiring to overturn the 2020 election. Each new incident or revelation has been taken by people outside the MAGA world as yet further confirmation of Trump's moral squalor and unfitness for office while leaving his followers within it largely unshaken.

Questions about Trump and January 6 once again elicited from most of his supporters reflexive denial of any reality that might reflect badly on him: He didn't lose the election, he's blameless for January 6, the Capitol invaders were his enemies in disguise, and despite all the indictments, he has never committed a crime.[33] To his most obdurate defenders, the Capitol invasion was peaceful and no police were hurt. The clearest tell is the 80 percent who said that the House hearings had not presented convincing evidence that Trump wanted to block certification of Biden's election despite Trump's loud, unequivocal, and fully documented demands for exactly that; they were not about to credit a pack of anti-Trump witch hunters for convincing them of anything that might make Trump appear blameworthy. For people who have invested time and again in the mental gymnastics required to defend Trump and to retain their own good opinion of him, the cumulative sunk costs make conceding that they might be wrong and his hated critics right prohibitively painful, particularly if most others in their social milieu remain Trump supporters; abandoning Trump would unsettle basic social identities.[34] The accounts of Trump's malfeasance that will be the focus of his multiple trials will offer yet another test of the power of motivated reasoning to protect Trump's standing with his MAGA supporters; after all that has gone before, there is no reason to think it will fail the test.

Democrats and Biden voters had their priors confirmed rather than challenged by January 6 and have not hesitated to condemn the rioters as criminals and terrorists, blame Trump for provoking the insurrection, and judge that both the rioters and Trump should be held criminally liable for their behavior. And their disdain goes beyond Trump and the rioters themselves: About 75 percent of Democrats and 79 percent of Biden voters think that "the Trump supporters who took over the Capitol building to stop Congressional proceedings represent most supporters of Donald Trump" (only 16 percent of Republicans and

---

[33] Less than a quarter of Republicans say that Trump committed any crime at any time as president or in his entire life (average, 23 percent across nine surveys asking these questions; survey sponsors 18, 19, and 31 in the Appendix).

[34] As Michael Lynch, a philosopher who studies the nature of political convictions, puts it, "To be blunt, Trump supporters aren't changing their minds because that change would require changing who they are, and they want to be that person" (quoted in Moritz 2023).

12 percent of Trump voters agree).[35] Democrats thus have some biased misperceptions of their own regarding January 6, as most Republicans and Trump voters have consistently said they did not support or approve of the Capitol invaders (recall Table 2).

2.3 How Did Trump Come to Command Such Loyalty?

Why did the assault on the Capitol, at first almost universally condemned, end up with the public dividing along familiar partisan lines in judging its inspirer? Why, specifically, did the great majority of Republicans reflexively take Trump's side in this as in every previous episode of questionable behavior?

2.3.1 Identity Politics

The primary answer lies in the powerful bonds of shared identity that Trump has forged with a core of set of MAGA followers large enough to dominate the Republican coalition. Trump had won the presidency in 2016 by exploiting right-wing populist resentment toward cultural, corporate, and political elites in both parties, conventional Republicans as well as Democrats. He offered himself as the champion of white Americans who felt besieged economically and culturally by globalism, immigration, feminism, secularism, and the growing racial and ethnic diversity of the country (Jacobson, 2017). Racial resentment and xenophobia in particular played no small part in his appeal (Abramowitz & McCoy, 2018; Hooghe & Dassonnevelle, 2018; Sides, Tesler, & Vavreck, 2018; Tesler, 2016). Heartened by his promises to "drain the swamp" in Washington DC and to make them feel like winners rather than losers, Trump's admirers proved willing to overlook his transparent lies and fantastic promises (e.g., having Mexico pay for a thirty-foot wall on the border), taking him "seriously but not literally." Trump expressed their sentiments in their language; his followers were amused rather than offended by his vulgar taunting of opponents, excited rather than put off by his authoritarian style and hints of violent retribution against their common enemies (Sides, Tesler, & Vavreck, 2018).

In office, Trump continued to give voice to the grievances, resentments, and illiberal opinions of (mainly) white middle- and working-class Americans facing a loss of political and cultural centrality and who feel, not without justification, ignored or belittled by Washington politicians, the corporate world, liberals quick to label them bigots, and the urban sophisticates in the media and entertainment industries (Jacobson, 2017, 2023b). Trump succeeded

---

[35] *Economist/* YouGov polls, June 2–8 and July 3–6, 2021, at https://today.yougov.com/topics/politics/explore/topic/The_Economist_YouGov_polls?content=surveys.

in persuading millions of disaffected Americans, less educated nonurban whites in particular, that he is on their side, that his enemies are their enemies, and that attacks on him are attacks on them, a message he continues to deliver in his campaign for redemption and reinstatement in 2024 as well as in diatribes against his indictments: "They're not indicting me, they're indicting you. I just happen to be standing in the way. Every time the radical left Democrats, Marxists, communists and fascists indict me, I consider it actually a great badge of honor ... Because I'm being indicted for you" (Calvin, 2023). Most of his supporters apparently agree; in a CBS News poll taken in August 2023 following his first three indictments, 56 percent of Republicans and 63 percent of Trump voters agreed with the proposition that "the indictments and investigations against Donald Trump are an attack on people like me."[36] It is doubtful that most of them really feel they risk prosecution for their politics, but the question provided an easy opportunity to declare solidarity with Trump.

The importance of white racial anxieties to Trump's appeal and support (Rhodes et al., 2022) is on full display in opinions regarding January 6. For example, the January 2021 American Perspective Survey[37] asked respondents their level of agreement with the statement, "discrimination against whites is as big a problem as discrimination against blacks." Seventy-two percent of Republicans agreed "somewhat" or "strongly," compared to 45 percent of independents and 14 percent of Democrats. Respondents were also asked about the accuracy of a series of statements regarding January 6. Republicans' positions on these questions were strongly related to their level of agreement with the racial discrimination statement (Figure 2). The more strongly Republicans believe that whites suffer as much discrimination as Blacks, the more likely they are to believe the big lie, absolve Trump, say the "deep state" was undermining him, blame antifa for the Capitol assault, believe the "QAnon" fantasy that Trump has been secretly battling a group of left-wing child sex traffickers (of which more in Section 2.6.2), as well as to hold a very favorable opinion of Trump.

Trump's successful appeal to white grievance and shared victimhood has served him well: People who see him as their ally and champion have a powerful incentive to adopt one or more modes of motivated reasoning, avoiding, ignoring, disbelieving, discounting, excusing, or dismissing as irrelevant anything suggesting that he might not deserve their support. To be sure, some portion of Trump's supporters appreciate him mainly for his policy goals and accomplishments – cutting corporate taxes and regulations, appointing conservative pro-life judges, confronting China on trade issues, pursuing

---

[36] CBS News Poll, August 2–4, 2023, www.scribd.com/document/663230100/cbsnews-20230806-1-SUN.

[37] www.americansurveycenter.org/download/jan-2021-american-perspectives-survey/.

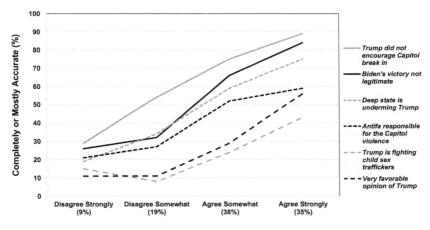

Figure 2 Republicans' views of discrimination against whites and beliefs about events related to January 6

a less interventionist foreign policy, beefing up border security, and overseeing a strong economy before COVID torpedoed it – sometimes despite strong reservations about his character and behavior. People backing Trump for pragmatic reasons face far less psychological pressure to buy any of his lies, including that of a stolen election, or to absolve him of blame for January 6 or for hiding classified documents at Mar-a-Lago. They simply have to tolerate his behavior as the price of getting their preferred policy outcomes. Some research suggests that the proportion of Trump supporters in this set is not large, however. A study that showed vignettes accurately describing six of Trump's questionable actions to a sample of his voters found that on average 47 percent said they would disapprove of the behavior but disbelieved the story in the vignette, 31 percent believed the story and approved of Trump's behavior, whereas only 11 percent believed the story while disapproving of Trump's behavior (Egan, 2023).[38] Using Egan's labels, "hear no evil" (selective exposure, motivated skepticism) evidently contributes far more than "hold your nose" pragmatism to preserving support for Trump.

---

[38] The remaining 9 percent didn't believe the story but supported Trump's described behavior anyway. The list of vignettes included his calling Mexican immigrants rapists, the Access Hollywood tapes, his denigration of some "shithole countries," the payoff to Stormy Daniels, his photo-op holding the Bible at a church near the White House, and his call for less COVID testing during the pandemic.

2.3.2 Demonizing the Democrats

Demonizing his opponents is integral to Trump's us-versus-them strategy, and, aided by an already highly polarized environment, it has largely succeeded. The partisan divide on issues and ideology among political elites, activists, and media entrepreneurs had been widening steadily over several decades before Trump emerged on the political scene. In Congress, for example, ideological divisions between the parties, party loyalty on divisive roll-call votes, and partisan differences in support for the president's agenda were reaching new highs as Trump announced his candidacy (Carson & Jacobson, 2023). Changes in the media ecosystem, notably the rise of Fox News and conservative talk radio and later the spread of social media had made public discourse more partisan, polarized, and contentions (Broockman & Kalla, 2023, Ding, Horning, & Rho 2023, Jurkowitz et al., 2020). Polarization has not been confined to politicians, activists, and pundits; Trump inherited an increasingly polarized electorate as well (Abramowitz, 2010; Abrams & Fiorina 2015; Campbell, 2016; Hetherington & Weiler, 2009; Jacobson, 2013; Lelkes, 2016; Levendusky, 2009) and then divided it further with crude attacks designed to excite fear and loathing of his Democratic opponents, exemplified by his attacks on "crooked Hillary" amid chants of "lock her up" in 2016 (Sides, Tausanovitch, &Vavreck, 2022, 50–56). The same rhetoric (along with many of his actions) amplified Democrats' fear and loathing of Trump and, by extension, his supporters. As a result, negative partisanship – a preference for one party driven largely by dislike of the other party and its leaders (Abramowitz & Webster, 2018; Fingerhut, 2018; Iyengar & Krupenkin, 2018; Martherus et al., 2021) – already on the upswing, intensified during Trump's presidency. Among Republicans, ratings of the Democratic Party on the ANES's 0–100 degree thermometer scale fell from an average of 34 degrees in 2012, to 29 degrees in 2016, and to 18 degrees in 2020; among Trump voters, it was down to 16 degrees, with 46 percent putting it at zero. Democrats' ratings of the Republican Party dropped similarly, from 30 degrees to 20 degrees over the same period, but the sharpest falloff was in their ratings of the Republican presidential candidate, from 29 degrees in 2012, to 15 degrees in 2016, and to frigid 7 degrees for Trump in 2020, with 76 percent choosing zero (American National Election Studies, 2022b).[39]

---

[39] Some of this drop in thermometer ratings derives from the ANES switching to a completely internet sample in 2020; the 2016 study, which used both telephone and internet samples, found that ratings of the rival party and candidate were three to five degrees lower in the latter. Thus, for example, Democrats' average rating of Trump in 2016 was eighteen degrees in the telephone sample and fifteen degrees in the internet sample. But even taking this difference into account, Trump's ratings in 2020 were far below that of any previous presidential candidate.

Partisans are now strongly disposed to see their rivals as distant and threatening. Responding to the 2020 postelection Pew survey, 81 percent of Trump voters and 77 percent of Biden voters said that they and the other side's voters "fundamentally disagree about core American values" (Deane & Gramlich, 2020; Pew Research Center, 2021). A pre-2022 election survey reported 81 percent of Democrats and 79 percent of Republicans saying they believed the other party's agenda would "pose a threat that if not stopped will destroy America as we know it" (Chinni, 2022; see also Cox, 2021). Insofar as Republicans have come to believe that Democrats pose an existential threat to their vision of the country and way of life, they are prepared to regard Democratic victories as inherently illegitimate (Serwer, 2020). If you believe Democratic leaders and their allies hate America and are bent on destroying it by imposing a socialist tyranny – a trope popular among far-right pundits and politicians ever since the Obama administration and eagerly adopted by Trump – election rigging is only to be expected. And fighting to overturn an election rigged by traitors is patriotism, not sedition.[40]

More generally, the growing coincidence of ideology, policy preferences, religiosity, and demography (race, gender, age, and education) with partisanship has made the party coalitions increasingly homogeneous internally and ideologically distant from one another (Abramowitz, 2010; Abrams & Fiorina, 2015). In concert with greater negative partisanship, this has produced what Sides, Tausanavitch, & Vavreck (2022) call the "calcification" of partisan politics. Fewer American than ever are now willing to vote for or approve of leaders in the other party. Hence, for example, party line voting set record highs and ticket-splitting set record lows in 2020 and 2022 (Jacobson, 2021b, 2023a), and the partisan gap in Gallup's presidential job approval ratings reached averages of eighty-one points for Trump and eighty points (so far) for Biden, notably wider than the seventy-one-point average for the next most divisive president, Barack Obama.[41] Polarization and calcified partisanship have worked to insulate Trump and, to a lesser extent, those who sought to overturn Biden's election on his behalf, from negative fallout over January 6 among ordinary Republicans. Regardless of Trump or his follower's transgressions, if any are conceded, Biden and the Democrats are worse – and, by the way, at greater fault for January 6 than Trump or congressional Republicans.

---

[40] Democratic leaders and pundits have yet to declare Republican victories as inherently illegitimate, although they do allege that Republican governors and legislators have been trying to rig their electoral systems to disadvantage Democratic voters.

[41] Calculated from data at Gallup's Presidential Job Approval Center, https://news.gallup.com/interactives/507569/presidential-job-approval-center.aspx.

2.3.3 Delegitimizing the News Media

Along with demonizing his Democratic opponents, Trump also prepared the ground for his followers' belief in the big lie (and innumerable smaller ones) and the rightness of his January 6 actions by portraying the mainstream news media as another common enemy. It was not a tough sell. Republicans' distrust of the news media had been growing for several decades before Trump exploited and then extended it through relentless attacks on mainstream journalists as "enemies of the people" peddling "fake news." Gallup documented a sharp decline in Republicans' "trust and confidence . . . in the mass media . . . reporting the news fully, accurately and fairly" during Trump's presidency; by September 2023, only 11 percent of Republicans were expressing "a great deal" or "a fair amount" of confidence in the news media, with 32 percent saying "not very much" and a remarkable 58 percent, "none at all" (Brennan, 2023). Responding to the fourteen Quinnipiac University polls taken during Trump's presidency that asked, "Who do you trust more to tell you the truth about important issues: President Trump or the news media?" an average of 78 percent of Republicans chose Trump and 13 percent chose the news media.[42] Most Trump supporters were thus fully primed to believe him rather than the mainstream journalists who tracked and shot down every specific claim of consequential election fraud, documented his and his allies' schemes to overturn the election, or reported on the classified documents illegally and carelessly cached at Mar-a-Lago.

2.3.4 Delegitimizing Other Institutions

Trump's impulse to delegitimize all critics and criticism has extended to any other institution attempting to hold him accountable, including the FBI, the Justice Department, and federal and state judiciaries and grand juries (Collins & Eshbaugh-Soha, 2023; Layne, 2023; Reich, 2023). Again, this has worked with ordinary Republicans. For example, the proportion of Republicans telling Gallup's interviewers that the FBI was doing an excellent or good job dropped from 59 percent in 2014 to 48 percent in 2019 and to 29 percent after the FBI raid at Mar-a-Lago in August 2022 (Jones, 2022; Younis, 2019).[43] Regarding the raid, only about a quarter of Republicans and Trump voters said it was true that "Trump was keeping sensitive national security documents at his home in Mar-a-Lago," while about half said it was true that "the FBI planted classified

---

[42] Quinnipiac Polls are available at https://poll.qu.edu/poll-results/.

[43] The FBI's actions had the opposite effect on Democrats, with the percentage assessing its performance as excellent or good rising from 61 percent in 2014 to 64 percent in 2019 and to 79 percent in 2022 (Jones 2022).

documents at former President Trump's home in Mar-a-Lago."[44] Asked if the "Justice Department's decision to indict Trump in the 2020 election subversion case was based on a fair evaluation of the evidence and the law," most Americans (59 percent) said yes, but 74 percent of Republicans disagreed, 47 percent "strongly."[45] In the June 2023 Fox News poll, only 32 percent of Republicans and 28 percent of Trump voters expressed even some confidence in the Justice Department.[46] Large Republican majorities consistently side with Trump in condemning his indictments as politically motivated.[47] Trump's pose as victim of unfair prosecution and martyr to his followers' cause has left them the choice between trusting him or the American justice system, and a large majority have sided with Trump.

2.3.5 Election Integrity

Like unbridled attacks on Democrats, critics, and the mainstream news media, election fraud charges are another Trump specialty that exploited preexisting Republican beliefs and sentiments. Despite its rarity, Republican politicians have long highlighted the threat of election fraud as justification for election "reforms" aimed at making it harder for Democratic-leaning groups (younger, lower income, and minority citizens) to vote (Anderson, 2019; Hajnal, Lajevardi, & Nielson, 2017; Johnson & Feldman, 2020). Trump amped up the fraud theme in 2016 by declaring Hillary Clinton's official 2.86 million popular vote margin bogus: "I won the popular vote if you deduct the millions of people who voted illegally" (Kessler, 2016). Republicans were inclined to believe him. Asked by the March 2017 Quinnipiac survey, "Do you believe that 3–5 million people voted illegally in the 2016 presidential election through widespread voter fraud, or not?" Fifty percent of Republicans said "yes," and 38 percent said "no."[48]

---

[44] *Economist*/YouGov polls, August 26–30 and September 3–6, 2022, at https://today.yougov.com/topics/politics/explore/topic/The_Economist_YouGov_polls?content=surveys.

[45] Eighty-nine percent of Democrats agreed, as did 64 percent if independents; Politico Magazine/Ipsos Survey, August 18–21, 2023, at www.ipsos.com/sites/default/files/ct/news/documents/2023-08/August%202023%20Politico%20Magazine%20Survey%20Trump%20Indictments.pdf.

[46] The figures for Democrats and Biden voters were 73 and 74 percent, respectively; https://static.foxnews.com/foxnews.com/content/uploads/2023/06/Fox_June-23-26-2023_Cross-Tabs_June-28-Release.pdf.

[47] For example, in the August 16–18, 2023, CBS News/YouGov poll, 77 percent of Republicans said the Georgia indictment was politically motivated, www.cbsnews.com/news/trump-poll-indictments-2023-08-20/.

[48] Quinnipiac Poll, March 16–21, 2017, accessed at https://poll.qu.edu/images/polling/us/us03222017_Upt839fm.pdf, July 12, 2022; 14 percent of Democrats and 24 percent of independents also said "yes."

In 2020, Trump alleged fraud well before the election took place, tweeting in June, for example, "RIGGED 2020 ELECTION: MILLIONS OF MAIL-IN BALLOTS WILL BE PRINTED BY FOREIGN COUNTRIES, AND OTHERS. IT WILL BE THE SCANDAL OF OUR TIMES!" (Budrik, 2020). Asked if they agreed or disagreed, 52 percent of Trump supporters agreed "strongly" and another 25 percent agreed "somewhat."[49] Heeding their leader, Trump's prospective voters grew to doubt that the election would be honest; on average, in the four Yahoo News/YouGov surveys taken between mid-September and mid-October 2020, only 22 percent anticipated a "fair and free election," while 47 percent did not.[50] Trump made it clear that he would refuse to accept any outcome that did not give him a second term, declaring in August, for example, that "the only way we are going to lose this election is if the election is rigged" (Chalfant, 2020). In the same four Yahoo News/YouGov surveys, an average of 60 percent of prospective Trump voters said they agreed with him. Well before the election, then, a strong majority of voters in Trump's camp were ready to deny the legitimacy of a Biden victory.

2.4 Opinion Leadership

Reactions of the MAGA world to Trump's defeat in 2020 and its aftermath were, then, deeply rooted in a set of political attitudes and beliefs that Trump had effectively exploited and reinforced during his presidency. In combination, they raised a formidable barrier against any second thoughts about the election and Trump that events of January 6 might have raised among his supporters. Whether opinion leaders in the Republican Party or conservative news media could have penetrated this barrier remains an open question because very few of them tried.

2.4.1 The News Media

Trump's partisans were accustomed to deflecting any negative information about their champion, and the impulse to protect their own extended to a considerable extent to cover the January 6 rioters. Mainstream news sources did try to keep the record straight but to little avail, not only because Trump's followers have come to despise and distrust them but also because plenty of alternative news outlets are available to people looking for affirmation of false beliefs. The stolen election and antifa claims have been tagged as "false" or

---

[49] Yahoo News/YouGov Race and Politics poll, June 24–25, 2020, https://docs.cdn.yougov.com/ove5ckbw84/20200626_yahoo_race_politics_crosstabs.pdf, July 17, 2022.
[50] Yahoo News/YouGov polls, September 15–17, October 1–2, October 9–11, and October 16–18, 2020.

"baseless" or "lacking evidence" in virtually every mainstream news story covering the events of January 6. The failure of these messages to change minds is consistent with research findings on how exposure to facts affects false beliefs. Nyhan (2021), reviewing this literature, argues that the "effects of corrective information like fact checks often do not last or accumulate" because they are "overwhelmed by cues from elites and the media promoting more congenial but less accurate claims." Most ordinary Americans don't pay a lot of attention to politics and form opinions on new political events and actors by relying on guidance from a few sources they have come to trust. If their sources misinform, they are misinformed. One obvious reason why false beliefs about January 6 persist is because they have continued to be promoted by Trump and his allies in politics and the media long after they have been thoroughly discredited.

"More congenial but less accurate claims" regarding January 6 and the events leading up to it have been widely available to Republicans and Trump voters from the start. Conservative news media, including the most influential by far, Fox News, provided a soapbox for the motley assortment of election deniers, with sympathetic hosts tacitly and sometimes openly endorsing their allegations as a way to humor and retain their audiences (Folkenflik, 2023). Fox eventually had to pay $787.5 million to settle a defamation suit brought by the voting machine vendor Dominion, a target of false election fraud charges leveled by several Fox hosts (Rutenberg, Schmidt, & Peters, 2023). The emails exposed by the suit showed that Fox executives and on-air talent knew the allegations were baseless but feared losing viewers to competitors if they said so (Peters & Robertson, 2023; Yang, 2023). Fox also promoted the antifa canard. As noted in Section 1, Tucker Carlson, then Fox News's top star, broadcast a three-part documentary in November 2021 alleging that the Capitol attack was not only a plot by leftists to discredit Trump but also a trap sprung by the FBI to justify jailing Trump supporters (McCarthy, 2021). This earned Fox another defamation suit, brought by the man Carlson alleged (and continues to allege) was the chief government *agent provocateur* on January 6 (Peters & Feuer, 2023).

Fox's fear of losing viewers was well founded (Ellison, Farhi, & Barr, 2023); if Fox balked at pandering to misinformed Trump supporters, they could find affirmation from less fastidious cable networks, such as the One America News Network or Newsmax, or from online charlatans who continue to promote a wide range of specious claims about January 6. Riling up audiences and monetizing their anger and gullibility has become a competitive business in which any good faith effort to report the facts would be a drag on the bottom line. The demand for congenial misinformation finds ready suppliers in the contemporary media ecosystem (Mir, 2020).

2.4.2 Republican Leaders

Trump supporters looking for affirmation of congenial misinformation about January 6 could also find ready suppliers among Republican elites. Like the conservative news media, most Republican leaders eventually yielded to their core constituency's demand for endorsement or at least indulgence of false beliefs about January 6 (Jacobson, 2023a: 162). The attack on the Capitol had given Republican leaders an opening to repudiate Trump and his big lie decisively and to end his political career by impeaching and convicting him. In the first days after the event, this seemed conceivable. Senate minority leader Mitch McConnell condemned Trump for inciting the attack and hinted that the offense might be impeachable (Raju et al., 2021). House minority leader Kevin McCarthy told colleagues he was going to advise Trump to resign and that impeachment was otherwise likely (Richards, 2022). Both blamed Trump directly for the Capitol invasion that had disrupted their work and put them in physical danger. Had they and other Republican leaders persisted in condemning Trump's lies and schemes and holding him accountable for invasion, at least some fraction of ordinary Republicans would have followed them, although millions of diehard MAGA enthusiasts certainly would not.

The opportunity for this field test of opinion leadership vanished when Republican leaders chose to appease their base rather than deliver unpalatable truths. Support for Trump and his big lie were simply too prevalent among their core voters to defy. Only a few hours after they had been driven from their respective chambers by the angry mob, 139 Republican representatives and eight senators voted against certifying the election results from at least one of the states Biden had won, and all but a handful of the rest subsequently declined to explicitly condemn the lie or the liar. Once it was clear where their partisans stood, senior Republican leaders backed away from any further steps to repudiate Trump. Within the month, McCarthy had made a pilgrimage to Mar-a-Lago to make obsequious peace with Trump, and even McConnell, though remaining a critic, pledged to support him if he were the 2024 nominee.

That Republican politicians and conservative media outlets felt compelled to indulge the false beliefs of their constituents and audiences raises questions about who influences whom. Do partisan leaders and media sources shape the beliefs of followers, or do followers compel opinion leaders who would retain that status to validate their beliefs? The answer is of course both: People rely on information sources they believe share their values and perspectives and who have in the past delivered messages deemed to be trustworthy; such opinion leader can subsequently shape their audiences thinking about new political actors or events. But once audiences have adopted the message and absorbed it into their view of reality, opinion leaders risk losing their trust and attention if they offer dissonant or contradictory information and thus may dissemble or remain silent rather than correct misperceptions. As the examples of Fox News and congressional Republicans suggest, it was the MAGA Republicans who held the upper hand after the 2020 election; most Republican politicians and their media allies felt it necessary to indulge their false beliefs rather than reveal their genuine and more accurate views of who won and what happened on January 6. These false beliefs did not arise spontaneously, to be sure. Trump's years of relentless attacks on the Washington "swamp," the mainstream news media, and election integrity, as well as his invocations of shared victimhood, had been taken to heart by his MAGA followers, priming them to accept his claims about what happened in the election and afterward. Anyone who wanted to remain in their good graces could not openly challenge Trump's big lie or hold him accountable for his postelection antics. In turn, silence or concurrence from trusted sources spared his followers messages that might have raised uncomfortable doubts, maintaining a dynamic of reciprocal reinforcement that continues to sustain false beliefs about the election and the events of January 6.

2.5 January 6 and the 2022 Midterm Election

The decision to stand with the base turned out to be politically prudent for congressional Republicans. At first, however, denying Biden's legitimacy and voting against certification appeared to be risky. The vote was not popular. A Quinnipiac survey taken in January 2021 asked respondents if "the Republican members of Congress who attempted to overturn the results of the 2020 presidential election should be celebrated for their actions or face consequences for their actions?" Overall, 22 percent chose "celebrated," while 63 percent chose "face consequences." The breakdown for Democrats was 2–94, and for independents, 23–62. About half of the Republicans (49 percent) said they should be celebrated, but 26 percent said they should face consequences. In the same poll, a solid majority of respondents thought those voting against certification were undermining rather than protecting democracy (58–34), including 90 percent of Democrats, 61 percent of independents, and 29 percent of Republicans.[51] Election denial was also generally unpopular; on average in the three 2022 preelection polls that asked, 11 percent of voters said they were more

---

[51] Quinnipiac Poll, January 7–10, 2021, https://poll.qu.edu/Poll-Release?releaseid=3733.

likely to vote for a candidate who said Trump had won, and 52 percent, less likely.[52] Campaign funding was also at risk; at least 231 corporations, including more than a hundred in the S&P 500 index, said they would suspend or reassess campaign contributions to members who voted against certification (Hernandez & Lash, 2023; Vachon, 2023).

In the end, however, it was not the deniers but rather those who insisted Biden won legitimately and sought to hold Trump accountable for January 6 who paid a political price. The handful of Republicans who had voted to impeach Trump and continued to call out his lie, notably Liz Cheney, became pariahs within the party; eight of the ten voting for impeachment were out of office by January 2023, four retiring and four, including Cheney, defeated by Trump supporters in primaries. Those who stuck with Trump did much better. Of the 181 House Republicans running for reelection in 2022, 111 had voted against certification. Two of them, Steve Chabot (OH 1st district) and Yvette Harrell (NM 3rd district) were the only Republican incumbents defeated in the 2022 general election, but they were primarily victims of redistricting in a year featuring record party line voting and continuity with the prior presidential vote.[53] Multivariate studies suggest that the electoral penalty for supporting Trump was very small to nonexistent. Bartels and Carnes (2023) found that voting against certification, against Trump's second impeachment, and/or against establishing a commission to investigate the Capitol invasion reduced neither vote shares nor the probability of winning. Jacobson (2023a) estimated that supporting the big lie cost Republican House incumbents a statistically significant ($p < 0.05$) but very small 1.0 percent of the vote; the effect of voting against certification alone was even smaller, 0.7 percent and only marginally significant ($p = 0.08$). One reason big lie supporters did not suffer at the polls is that two-thirds of the corporations that had pledged to reconsider donating to members who voted against certification ended up contributing to them after all (Hernandez & Lash, 2023; Vachon, 2023); statistically, a vote against certification or denial of Biden's legitimacy had no significant effect on either their own or their opponent's financial support.[54]

---

[52] NBC News polls, May 5–10 and October 14–18, 2022; Quinnipiac Poll, October 26–30, 2022.

[53] Biden's share was 48.4 percent in Chabot's old district, 54.3 percent in his new district, for Harrell, Biden's share increased from 44.4 percent to 51.9 percent after redistricting. The correlation in 2022 between the House vote and the lagged district presidential vote was 0.983, and 94.7 percent of seats went to the party with a local presidential majority, both all time highs for a midterm election (Jacobson, 2023a).

[54] Regressing logged campaign spending by and for Republican incumbents or by and for their opponents on the certification vote, controlling for district partisanship as estimated by the presidential vote in 2020, produced small, statistically insignificant coefficients on the certification vote.

This is not to say the January 6 invasion and Trump's meddling in nomination politics to help election deniers was entirely inconsequential. Controlling for the 2020 district presidential vote and campaign spending, nonincumbent Republican House candidates endorsed by Trump ran about 3 percentage points below expectations, as did his Senate endorsees (Abramowitz, 2023; Jacobson, 2023a). It is doubtful that the endorsement itself turned off voters; more likely, the candidates not already in office who were willing to do what it took to win Trump's endorsement were on average simply less talented and appealing candidates. Support for the big lie had no statistical effect in these House races, but the seven Republican candidates for statewide offices charged with managing elections and the five nonincumbent Republican candidates for governor who denied Biden's legitimacy ran 4–6 points worse than local partisanship would predict, and all twelve lost; the only two deniers who won governorships were incumbents in deep red states, Idaho and Alabama (Jacobson, 2023a). Malzahn and Hall (2023) also found that election deniers underperformed in statewide elections. Election denial was clearly not a winning stance for new office seekers in 2022, but Bartels and Carnes (2023) are on solid ground in concluding that voters did not, in aggregate, punish Republican members of Congress for trying to disrupt the lawful transfer of power following a presidential election even after witnessing the Capital mayhem on January 6.

Calcified partisanship puts a huge premium on turnout, and if January 6 did any general damage to Republicans in 2022, it was mainly by encouraging Democrats who were unhappy with Biden and the inflationary economy to show up anyway to cast a vote, as they had in 2018 and 2020, against Trumpism. A greater stimulus, though, was Democrats' anger at the Supreme Court's *Dobbs* decision ending nearly fifty years of constitutional protection for abortion rights (Carson & Ulrich, 2024; Jacobson, 2023a). High Democratic turnout kept the election from being a straightforward referendum on the economy and Biden's performance, depriving Republicans of an anticipated "red wave" (Jacobson, 2023a). Some Republican leaders blamed Trump for their disappointing showing and were less than thrilled when he announced his 2024 candidacy nine days after the election (Goodwin, 2022). Their grumbling was, as usual, mostly anonymous for fear of antagonizing pro-Trump Republican voters.

2.6 Additional Effects and Implications of January 6

Reactions to the events of January 6 have a variety of additional consequences and implications for American politics going forward. They include further polarization, a Republican coalition that now openly includes devotees of bizarre conspiracy theories, and the specter of political violence.

2.6.1 More Polarization

The January 6 Capitol assault fueled another round in the vicious cycle of polarization that has marked the Trump era. First, it gave Democrats and other Trump critics yet more reason to despise him, confirming once again his mendacity, recklessness, authoritarian instincts, and utter disrespect for American institutions – judgments were only reinforced by his behavior after January 6. Trump doubled down on the big lie, notoriously demanding more than a year after the election that he be declared the rightful winner or that a new election be held because a "Massive Fraud of this type and magnitude allows for the termination of all rules, regulations, and articles, even those found in the Constitution" (Astor, 2022). He also promised "full pardons and an apology to many" of the Capitol invaders who have pleaded or been found guilty for their actions (Alfalo, 2022).

Second, the worse Trump looks to his detractors, the worse they think of his Republican supporters (Harris, 2020). How can you respect the intelligence, judgment, or good faith of people willing to endorse Trump's self-serving lies, deny or justify his schemes to disenfranchise millions of voters, excuse or trivialize the violence and destructiveness of his supporters at the Capitol, and refuse to hold him or them accountable for it? The sense of being disrespected by educated liberals in the Democratic Party, academia, entertainment, and the mainstream media that originally drove less educated, socially conservative whites toward the MAGA movement gained a new measure of reality after January 6 (e.g., Marcotte, 2023).

Third, people looking for reasons to continue to back Trump despite the cumulative evidence of his unfitness for office find it ever more imperative to view his opponents as evil and dangerous: Trump may have his flaws, but Biden and the Democrats are worse, and Republicans are even more united in disliking them than in liking Trump. In the *Economist*/YouGov weekly surveys taken in 2023, 78 percent of Republican identifiers had very (48 percent) or somewhat (30 percent) favorable opinions of Trump, while 89 percent had very (79 percent) or somewhat (10 percent) unfavorable opinions of Biden, and 87 percent had very (69 percent) or somewhat (18 percent) unfavorable views of the Democratic Party ($N = 28,179$). Even among Republicans who viewed Trump unfavorably, 78 percent had very (59 percent) or somewhat (19 percent) unfavorable opinions of Biden. Biden has become an object of scorn for right-wing politicians and pundits, led by the Fox News lineup, who attack him relentlessly as senile, incompetent, an America-hating socialist, and, directly and through his wayward son Hunter, corrupt. Attacking Biden is easier than coming up with plausible defenses of Trump's more outrageous actions (hiding classified documents in insecure locations, bullying Georgia officials to falsify vote totals, etc.) and demands ("termination" of constitutional rules preventing his immediate reinstatement) and serves to keep their audiences anxious, indignant, and engaged. House speaker McCarthy similarly embraced strategic distraction when, after Trump's indictments, he bowed to the demand of the hard-right Freedom Caucus and initiated an impeachment inquiry targeting Biden even though a lengthy Oversight Committee investigation had failed to produce any credible evidence of malfeasance (Smith, 2023).

Aware of how much his support depends on hatred of his adversaries, Trump has pushed his rhetorical assaults on Biden and the Democrats to hysterical extremes. At a campaign rally in Waco in March 2023, for example, he denounced Biden administration officials as "thugs and criminals" who have created "a Stalinist horror show" by "weaponizing" the Justice Department against him. He charged that "the abuses of power that are currently with us at all levels of government will go down as among the most shameful, corrupt and depraved chapters in all of American history." He described the US under Biden as becoming a "third world banana republic," and as "a nation in decline … a joke … a nation that is hostile to liberty, freedom, and faith." Moreover, he is just the rule-breaking tough guy needed to thwart the evil forces threatening them and theirs: "I am your warrior. I am your justice. For those who have been wronged and betrayed, I am your retribution." And, "together, we are taking on some of the most menacing forces and vicious opponents our people have ever seen. … But no matter how hateful and corrupt the communists and criminals we're fighting against may be, you must never forget, this nation does not belong to them – this nation belongs to you."[55]

Demonizing opponents and invoking shared victimhood is vintage Trump, but he reached weird new heights as his legal jeopardy escalated,[56] contributing, like the events of January 6 themselves, to ever deeper partisan divisions in American society. As noted earlier, affective polarization – mutual disdain between Democrats and Republicans – set new records during Trump's presidency and has continued to grow since January 6. This was not the only possibility. It is not

---

[55] Quotes are from a transcript of Trump's March 25, 2023 speech in Waco, Texas, available at www.rev.com/blog/transcripts/donald-trump-hosts-first-2024-presidential-campaign-rally-in-waco-texas-transcript.

[56] In August 2023, for example, Trump shared an article on his Truth Social platform that claimed that if he did not win in 2024, Republicans and conservatives would be outlawed and enslaved (Wolf 2023).

entirely fanciful to imagine that a violent assault on the nation's Capitol would be sobering enough to spur at least some movement toward a national detente in recognition of a shared stake in American democracy. In reality, however, the events of January 6 have had the opposite effect, and partisan acrimony promises to get only nastier as the 2024 campaigns ramp up while Trump defends himself against criminal charges in multiple courtrooms.

2.6.2 Mainstreaming Extremism

The stated beliefs and opinions of ordinary Republicans about events surrounding January 6, reviewed in Section 1, help map out the Republican coalition that has emerged since Trump's hostile takeover of the party in 2016. The most extreme faction consists of hard-core Trump supporters, comprising perhaps a third of Republican identifiers, who express some combination of positive views of the Capitol invaders, belief that their actions were justified and not violent or, alternatively, that the invasion was a false-flag plot to discredit Trump, and belief that Mike Pence was wrong to count the electoral votes on January 6.[57] They absolve Trump of all blame for the mayhem and are firmly committed to the big lie, for which they claim "solid evidence."

This faction is open to other conspiracy theories. For example, among Republicans in the December 2021 Ipsos poll, not only did 23 percent say it was true that the Capitol invaders were "Antifa and government agents," but 21 percent said it was true that COVID-19 "was planned by a group of global elites, as a way of controlling the population," and 11 percent said it was true that "a group of Satan-worshipping elites who run a child sex ring are trying to control our politics and media." Believers in one of these conspiracies are much more likely to believe in another. For example, 59 percent of believers in the antifa conspiracy also said that elites planned the COVID pandemic, compared to 8 percent of nonbelievers; 40 percent of antifa believers also endorsed the child sex ring conspiracy, compared to 2 percent of nonbelievers.[58]

The "QAnon" notion that "Donald Trump has been secretly fighting a group of child sex traffickers that include prominent Democrats and Hollywood elites" was supported by an even larger share of Republicans in the January 2021 American Perspectives Survey, 27 percent. Similarly, three Public Religion Research Institute (PRRI) surveys taken between May 2021 and

---

[57] Responding to three surveys that asked if Pence had the authority to block certification or should have done so, an average of 31 percent of Republicans said he did or should have, with 41 percent taking the opposition positions (Quinnipiac Poll, February 10–14, 2022; CBS/YouGov Poll, August 16–18, 2023; *Economist*/YouGov poll, August 26–29, 2023).

[58] Ipsos Poll December 3–7, 2021, Roper Center Dataset, https://doi.org/10.25940/ROPER-31119144.

September 2022 found an average of 26 percent of Republicans subscribing to a set of three QAnon-related beliefs.[59] A slightly smaller fraction (averaging 23 percent) said that it was at least somewhat likely that "Donald Trump will be re-instated as President before the end of 2021" when asked about this prospect – floated by Trump among others – in the twelve weekly *Economist*/YouGov polls taken from August through October 2021. Eighteen percent were still considering Trump's reinstatement a possibility as time ran out in December, although it is most doubtful that these were genuine beliefs as opposed to wishful fantasies or simply trolling the pollsters. The reported incidence of QAnon beliefs is also exaggerated by contrarian posturing and measurement flaws (Clifford, Kim, & Sullivan, 2019; Enders et al., 2022), but millions of Americans – including some House Republicans – are evidently willing to endorse even the most absurd notions if they malign Democrats and cast Trump in a favorable light (Tully-McManus, 2020).

The January 6 mob was drawn largely from this extreme faction, which is a stable if not growing component of the Republican coalition. Politicians and pundits catering to its views have brought ugly conspiracy-based allegations into right-wing discourse (Rosenberg, 2020). Echoing QAnon, Republican candidates presenting as culture warriors have added to their repertoires charges that their opponents support "grooming" children for sexual exploitation (Itkowitz, 2022; Sommer, 2023; Thompson, 2022). Elise Stefanik, a Republican from upstate New York who is currently chair of the House Republican Conference, has lumped Democrats with "pedo grafters" while also endorsing another conspiracy theory, the so-called "great replacement," that has migrated from the white supremacist netherworld into the Republican mainstream (Bauder, 2022; Karni, 2022). Although it takes various forms, the key claim is that leftists and globalists (the Democratic Party, big corporations, and, in its anti-Semitic variant, Jews) are conspiring to flood the voter rolls with compliant non-white immigrants who will permanently outvote "traditional" Americans (i.e., conservative Christian whites). The theory evidently makes sense to many Trump supporters; responding to a May 2022 Yahoo News/YouGov poll, 61 percent of Trump voters agreed strongly (31 percent) or somewhat (30 percent) that "a group of people in this country are trying to replace native-born Americans with immigrants and people of color who share

---

[59] The PRRI measures QAnon belief based on agreement with three statements: (1) The government, media, and financial worlds in the US are controlled by a group of Satan-worshipping pedophiles who run a global child sex-trafficking operation; (2) there is a storm coming soon that will sweep away the elites in power and restore the rightful leaders; and (3) because things have gotten so far off track, true American patriots may have to resort to violence in order to save our country (Huff, 2022; PRRI Staff, 2021).

their political views." Belief in the stolen election lie and the great replacement overlap, with 75 percent of Republicans who thought the 2020 election was "fraudulent, rigged and illegitimate" also agreeing at least somewhat with the great replacement theory (Romano, 2022).

This hard-core faction has of course been all in for Trump in the face of his felony indictments. It would be included in the slightly larger share of Republicans, 37 percent, classified in the July 2023 *New York Times*/Sienna poll as MAGA enthusiasts, defined as respondents who strongly support Trump in the primaries and hold a very favorable view of him. Nate Cohn reports the astonishing finding that "zero percent – not a single one of the 319 respondents in this MAGA category – said he had committed serious federal crimes. A mere 2 percent said he 'did something wrong' in his handling of classified documents." Cohn's conclusion: "The MAGA base doesn't support Mr. Trump in spite of his flaws. It supports him because it doesn't seem to believe he has flaws" (Cohn, 2023) – or at least none admitted in response to a survey. Such seemingly boundless loyalty has convinced some observers that Trump and his MAGA following constitute a classic cult (Hassan, 2020; Lewis 2021; Sagal 2023).

2.6.3 The Never Trumpers and Other Republicans

A second faction that forms a rather smaller portion of Republican identifiers, 20–25 percent, holds the opposite views of Trump and the Capitol rioters. It includes Republicans who say the insurgents were criminals or domestic terrorists trying to keep Trump power, were engaged in insurrection rather than legitimate political discourse, and were neither antifa nor FBI provocateurs. These Republicans supported the House hearings on events of January 6, believe Biden won legitimately, hold Trump responsible for January 6, think he provoked violence, and believe he sought to overturn the election and should be prosecuted for doing so. They correspond to the approximately one-quarter of the Republican electorate in Cohn's analysis who won't consider voting for Trump in a primary or even a general election, although they might just stay home rather than voting for Biden (Cohn, 2023). Only a tiny proportion of this faction endorses any of the conspiracy theories that animate many in the first faction.

A third, more amorphous set of Republicans are neither all in for Trump nor done with him. They join with the MAGA faction to make up the overall Republican majorities saying the attackers were engaged in legitimate discourse, were patriots, were being punished too severely, and should be pardoned – or else that they were leftists and antifa. They also contributed to the majorities who deny Biden's legitimacy and Trump's responsibility for January 6, who were critical of the House hearings, and who don't want Trump prosecuted. On the other hand, they join with Trump's critics within the party to make up the large majority disapproving of the attackers and their actions as well as the narrower majority that wants them held accountable. They contributed to the plurality that say Pence did the right thing in certifying Biden's victory on January 6. They also join in the broader Republican rejection of QAnon and associated crank conspiracy theories.

The two polar factions have different demographic compositions. On average, the hard-core MAGA faction is older, less educated, lower income, more rural, and more conservative. The anti-Trump faction is wealthier, better educated, more urban or suburban, and more moderate. The middle faction falls, appropriately, in the middle on these dimensions. The "always Trumpers" outnumber the "never Trumpers" but the middle faction holds the balance of voting power within the party. Some evidence suggests this middle faction edged away from Trump in the aftermath of January 6. Since January 2020, the NBC News/*Wall Street Journal* polls have at intervals asked Republican identifiers if they considered themselves more Trump supporters or more Republican Party supporters. Trump lost ground relative to the party after the Capitol invasion (Figure 3), although about one-third continue to consider themselves primarily Trump supporters – the "always Trumpers" again. Still, Trump remains popular even among most Republicans who put the party first, and going into the winter of 2024 remains the overwhelming favorite among Republican primary voters.[60]

2.7 The Republicans' Dilemma in 2024

Looking toward the 2024 general election, the challenge for Republican leaders is to keep the MAGA Republicans on board and engaged while competing effectively for the votes of other Republicans, independent voters, and potential Democratic defectors. Trump's insistence on the stolen election lie, his increasingly warm embrace of the Capitol invaders (Carter, 2023), and his multiple indictments make the latter considerably more difficult. For the primary season, pleasing the MAGA Republicans has been taking precedence. Loyalty to Trump and the big lie and denunciation of his indictments have become something of a litmus test for Republican candidates, and most of Trump's rivals for the nomination, coveting his MAGA following, have criticized him only obliquely

---

[60] Twice as many Republicans expressed positive views of Trump as put him ahead of the party on this question in the June 2023 NBC News/*Wall Street Journal* poll, www.documentcloud.org/documents/23863177-230169-nbc-june-2023-poll-final-release.

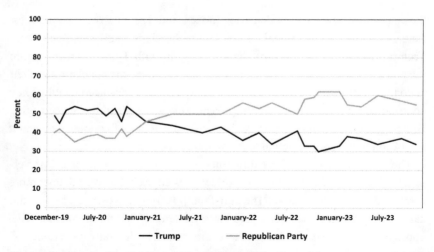

Figure 3 Asked of Republicans: Do you consider yourself more a supporter of
Trump or more a supporter of the Republican Party?
(NBC News/*Wall Street Journal* Polls)

if at all. Six of the eight participants in the first Republican debate of the 2024
election cycle in August 2023, including Ron DeSantis and Mike Pence,
promised to back Trump even if he is convicted of a felony; only two considered
his indictments (and the actions that led to them) as reasons to oppose his
nomination (Piper, 2023).[61] Tellingly, the combined support in primary election
polls for the six loyalists in the month after the debate averaged 34 percent,
compared to 4 percent for the two Trump critics. Of course, candidates who
condemn the indictments, oppose holding Trump accountable, and praise most
of his achievements as president struggle to explain why people should vote for
them rather than him; Trump's share in these polls was 54 percent.[62]

With few exceptions, other Republican leaders have also criticized the
indictments rather than Trump. They can't be unaware of Trump's unpopular-
ity outside Republican circles and the problem his presence on the ballot
would pose for them in the general election.[63] But they also have to worry
that if they did manage to deny Trump the nomination, a large slice of his
MAGA base might sit out the election, hurting the party in downballot races
and handing Congress to the Democrats. Their quandary: What is worse for

---

[61] The other candidates who said they would vote for Trump were Nikki Haley, Tim Scott, Vavek
Ramaswamy, and Doug Burgum; the two Trump critics were Chris Christie and Asa Hutchinson.
[62] https://projects.fivethirtyeight.com/polls/president-primary-r/2024/national/.
[63] In *Economist*/YouGov surveys taken since Trump's indictments, 79 percent of respondents who
did not identify as Republicans have expressed unfavorable opinions of him, and 68 percent,
very unfavorable ($N = 11,278$).

the party in 2024, Trump on the ticket or Trump not on the ticket? Most would probably prefer a ticket without Trump – who is, after all, a uniquely potent mobilizer of Democratic voters (Jacobson, 2019a, 2019b, 2021b, 2023a) – in order to focus the 2024 election campaign on the unpopular Joe Biden's performance and policies, but only if they can derail a Trump nomination without alienating his supporters, which at this point, absent some exogenous bombshell, does not seem possible.

2.8 January 6 as a Stress Test for American Democracy

The events surrounding the January 6 Capitol invasion tested and, with the cases now before the courts, will continue to test the strength and resilience of American democracy. The scheming by Trump and his confederates to overturn a fair and free election despite the total absence of evidence that the official results from any state did not accurately reflect the voters' choices was a direct assault on its foundations. So was the invasion of the Capitol by a mob hoping to keep Trump in office by blocking certification of Biden's victory. Had they and Trump succeeded, the world's oldest democracy would have suffered its first coup d'état. That they did not succeed and are being prosecuted for trying to attest to the resilience of American institutions. It also raises the question of how serious the threat actually was and how resilient these institutions will remain going forward.

2.8.1 Who Defended Democracy?

Postwar researchers, haunted by the ruinous collapse of some European democracies in the prewar period, developed a theory that democracy's survival depends on political elites: Politicians and activists, schooled by training and experience in the norms and habits of democratic politics, would uphold democratic principles when they come under threat – perhaps from mass publics less committed to them (e.g., McClosky & Brill, 1983; Stouffer, 1955; for a review article, see Peffley & Rohrschneider, 2009). The theory has been challenged from a number of directions over the years but still provides a useful starting point for considering the current health of American democracy. If the maintenance of democracy depends on political elites, how well did they perform in 2020? We can set aside Democratic elites because upholding democracy coincided with their own immediate political interests, leaving their commitments untested. Republican elites did face a conflict and so a test. Those who endorsed Trump's specious claims of a stolen election joined his intrigues to overturn the results and justified or excused his behavior before and after January 6 have clearly failed it. Only the most delusional among them can actually believe the stolen election lie; the rest simply prefer to propitiate Trump and his MAGA following and hold onto power regardless of the damage to American democracy.

The 147 congressional Republicans who voted against certifying Biden's election are also arguably among those who failed the test, but the vote was not actually a clean test. With Democrats controlling the House and most Republican senators clearly unwilling to join them, they knew for certain their votes could not actually block certification. Suppose they had been in a position to reverse the election's outcome, disenfranchising millions of voters on the flimsiest of pretexts: Would they have done it? I suspect most would have drawn back from that precipice, not wanting history to remember them for such a dubious achievement. As it was, the vote against certification was pure position taking – pleasing to their voters but guaranteed to be futile, neither overturning the election nor creating a constitutional chaos by delaying certifi-cation. A disinclination to nullify the election was evident in common explan-ations of the vote; they were not voting to overturn the election but only to recheck the results to address allegations of fraud and to reassure constituents who believed the election had been stolen (Behrmann & Santucci, 2021). Their electoral fates in 2022 confirmed the efficacy of this approach and also showed that ordinary voters could not be counted on to punish breaches of basic democratic norms (Bartels & Carnes, 2023), a result anticipated by experimen-tal evidence that in a polarized environment, only a small fraction of the electorate would put support for democratic principles ahead of party and ideology (Graham & Svolik, 2020). But 2022 was not a clean test for Republican voters either, because belief in the stolen election lie cast the effort to overturn the results in a pro- rather than anti-democratic light.

Since Trump's election in 2016, self-preservation has kept most congres-sional Republicans from breaking with him, underlining the futility of expecting people who rely on votes for their jobs to act on principle if it requires defying a strong consensus among the people who keep them in office. Thus, the Republican elites who did actively resist Trump's assault on democratic norms and procedures were not, with a few honorable exceptions, found in Congress. Republican governors, secretaries of state, and local election officials in disputed states (Georgia, Arizona, and Nevada) did strongly defend the integrity of their states' elections, not only because they knew firsthand that the votes had been properly processed and counted, but also because managing the election had been their responsibility; bowing to pressure by Trump and his allies to nullify the results would have meant admitting to incompetence and failure. Many Republican legislators (44 percent by one count) in disputed states where their party controlled both chambers did vote to overturn the results, but these efforts were blocked, where necessary, by Republican colleagues who joined the Democrats in refusing to go along (Cheney, 2020; Corasaniti, Yourish, & Collins, 2022). Senior Trump appointees in the Justice Department and other federal agencies, notably attorney general Robert Barr, also firmly resisted pressure to challenge official state results on specious claims of fraud (H.R. Rep. No. 117–613, 2022: 373–403). And of course Vice President Pence ultimately refused to be bullied into ignoring the law and Constitution to keep Trump in power. However, the most sustained elite and institutional defense of American democracy took place in the courts, where judges from both parties, including some Trump appointees, rejected virtually every challenge to election results mounted by Trump and his allies by simply applying conventional judicial standards of evidence, law, and standing (Danforth et al., 2022).

2.8.2 The Indictments

Law enforcement agencies and courts have also taken the lead in holding the January 6 Capitol invaders accountable and are now engaged in prosecuting Trump and his confederates for attempting to overturn the election. These efforts have generally divided the public along partisan lines familiar from reactions to other issues surrounding January 6 reported in Section 1, but at least initially, the formal indictments have been followed by some small but marginally significant shifts in public opinion in favor of holding Trump legally liable for his actions. Table 21 reports levels of support for prosecuting Trump and/or deeming him guilty before and after the indictments were delivered.[64] Support for prosecuting Trump in the election interference and classified documents cases was higher after the indictments among voters in all categories, excepting only Biden voters in the documents case. The differences pre- and post-indictment for the elections cases are significant at $p < .05$ or better for all groups except Trump voters ($p = 0.424$).[65] The documents case saw the largest shift in favor of prosecution among Republicans and Trump voters, who seem more inclined to take these charges seriously than the election interference charges.[66] In contrast, support for the hush money

---

[64] The federal and Georgia indictments for conspiring to overturn election results are combined because popular responses to each are virtually identical; only one hush money poll preceded the indictment, so not enough "before" data are available for comparison in this set.

[65] Estimated by regressing the percentage of support for prosecution for each subgroup on a categorical variable indicating the survey was taken post-indictment, with survey sponsor fixed effects.

[66] The differences between pre- and post-indictment are significant at the $p < 0.06$ level or less for all categories except Biden voters.

Table 21 Support indictments/consider Trump guilty (percent)

	All		Democrats		Independents		Republicans	
	Yes	No	Yes	No	Yes	No	Yes	No
For attempt to overturn 2020 election (Federal and Georgia cases)								
Before indictments (41)	48	40	82	9	45	38	12	78
After indictments (22)	52	36	86	7	52	32	16	73
For mishandling classified documents								
Before indictment (9)	48	39	82	9	46	38	12	76
After indictment (17)	53	36	85	9	52	33	19	69
For falsifying business records – Stormy Daniels hush money (17)	49	34	81	8	46	32	18	66

	Biden voters		Trump voters	
	Yes	No	Yes	No
For attempt to overturn 2020 election (Federal and Georgia cases)				
Before indictments (26)	86	7	8	84
After indictments (9)	90	4	9	82
For mishandling classified documents				
Before indictment (6)	87	6	8	81
After indictment (6)	85	11	17	70
For falsifying business records – Stormy Daniels hush money (8)	81	8	11	73

Note: The number of polls averaged is in parentheses.
Source: Surveys 1, 2, 5–7, 9, 12, 13, 15, 16, 18, 19, 20, 23, 24, and 27 listed in the Appendix.

indictment is a few points lower across the board, and fewer people deem these charges "very" serious.[67]

2.8.3 Democracy under Threat in 2024

Whether the modest post-indictment bump in support for prosecuting Trump will be sustained through the election year amid the multiple ongoing judicial proceedings remains uncertain. Whatever happens, American electoral institutions will certainly be tested anew by the potential for confusion, chaos, and violent discord as Trump and his allies mount simultaneous campaigns to win the nomination, the White House, and acquittal in four separate courts of law, while Democrats are working to assure that he loses the election and prosecutors, the cases.

The threats to American democracy manifest on January 6 and continuing in its aftermath have led some prominent scholars of American politics to question its health and durability, with or without Trump on the scene (Aldrich et al., 2021; Fields, 2023; Hasen, 2022; Leonhardt, 2022; Levitsky & Ziblatt, 2023; Walter, 2022; for a more sanguine analysis, see Weyland, 2020). Many ordinary Americans share their concerns. For example, 69 percent of both Democratic and Republican respondents to an August 2022 Quinnipiac poll said that "the nation's democracy is in danger of collapse."[68] Seventy-one percent of voters in the October 2022 *New York Times*/Sienna poll agreed that "American democracy is currently under threat," including 74 percent of Democrats and 72 percent of Republicans.[69] Of course, bipartisan consensus vanishes when people are asked to specify the source of the threat; partisans say it comes from the other party, its leaders, allies, and policies, illustrating one of the main reasons people worry about American democracy's future – deep partisan divisions.[70]

---

[67] For example, in the September 7–11, 2023, Quinnipiac, 51 percent said the charges in documents case were very serious, and 14 percent, somewhat serious. The respective figures for the federal elections case were 54 and 9 and for the Georgia case, 53 and 12, but for the hush money case, they were 33 and 23, https://poll.qu.edu/poll-release?releaseid=3878.

[68] https://poll.qu.edu/Poll-Release?releaseid=3831.

[69] www.nytimes.com/interactive/2022/10/18/upshot/times-siena-poll-registered-voters-crosstabs.html.

[70] For example, responding to the December 2022 NPR/Marist College poll, 83 percent of respondents, including 86 percent of Democrats and 83 percent of Republicans, said "issues that divide the nation" were "a serious threat to the future of our democracy"; but 84 percent of Democrats and 80 percent of Republicans regarded the other party as the predominant source of the threat, https://maristpoll.marist.edu/wp-content/uploads/2022/11/NPR_PBS-NewsHour_Marist-Poll_USA-NOS-and-Tables_202210281214.pdf.

2.8.4 More Political Violence?

Contributing to the anxiety is the specter of political violence raised by the assault on the Capitol. Survey studies of popular support for political violence detected an increase after January 6, with some reporting that a third or more of the public now endorse at least some forms of intimidation or violence against political opponents (Cox, 2021; Kalmoe & Mason, 2022; Klienfeld, 2022; Thompson-DeVeaux, 2022). Other studies report considerably lower support for political violence (Jackson, 2022), with the lowest reported by Westwood et al. (2022), who argue that ambiguous questions and respondent disengagement have led to gross overestimates. Their experimental studies, designed to correct these faults, estimate the percentage of Americans who genuinely support physical violence against opponents to be in the low single digits. Still, their median estimate of 2.9 percent amounts to 7.7 million adults, more than enough to supply legions of foot soldiers for the kind actions witnessed on January 6. What will Trump's more bellicose supporters do if he is convicted and sentenced or loses in 2024 and again claims the election was stolen?

Although January 6 set a precedent for violent action on Trump's behalf, that precedent also includes the unhappy fates of the Capitol invaders. The suspicion that they were victims of FBI entrapment also gives pro-Trump militants reason to be wary of involvement in anything similar (Feuer, 2023b). So far, outrage at Trump's indictments has sparked numerous threats of violent retaliation against people involved in his prosecution but little else. Death threats against judges, grand jurors, and prosecutors have exploded on the Internet, as have calls to arms and allusions to civil war, some endorsed by far-right Republican politicians (Day, Kahn, & Loadenthal, 2023; Elving, 2022; Pengelly, 2023; Schmidt et al., 2023b). The threat of individual violence targeting Trump's purported enemies is palpable and alarming, but collective action to protest his indictments has been minimal. Despite Trump's predictions of "potential death & destruction" were he to be indicted, the courthouse protests he has called for have so far been small and peaceful (Blake, 2023; Feuer, 2023b; Silverman & Allam, 2023).

Even if Trump loses but claims victory again in 2024, a repeat of anything like January 6 assault on the Capitol seems very unlikely. Law enforcement will not be caught off guard, and anyone identified as the leader of a group given to violent protests can expect to be under heavy surveillance. Would-be insurgents will have a clear picture of the potential consequences. They might also be more realistic about their chances of success. The idea of the Capitol invasion as a "1776" moment as imagined by some of the invaders (H.R. Rep. No. 117–613, 2022: 639) looks utterly delusional in hindsight. The expectation that they could force Congress to overturn a presidential election, effectively executing a coup d'état on Trump's behalf, with nothing close to adequate numbers, arms, popular support, or assistance from the police, military, and courts seems remarkably naïve. Trump certainly did not command the authority or institutional backing to alter that equation on January 6, and full-throated endorsement of the insurgency would have only assured his impeachment. The insurgents were fortunate that January 6 did not turn into a much bloodier affair, a real possibility had they seized Pence, Pelosi, or other members of Congress, as some intended (H.R. Rep. No. 117–613, 2022: 641–642), or if they had fought to hold the building. If Trump's convictions or another lost election were to provoke further organized violence on his behalf in 2024 – by no means out of the question given the mentality and arsenals of some MAGA extremists (Schmidt et al., 2023a) – it will, I think, have to take a very different form. Whatever form it takes, the prison sentences of up to twenty-two years handed down to those convicted of seditious conspiracy for their roles in January 6 are likely to discourage all but the most militant and reckless from participating.

2.8.5 The Decision in 2024

Although the chances of another Capitol insurrection or some other violent coup attempt are remote, that does not mean that American democracy is not under threat. The threat comes from an electorate that might actually send Donald Trump back to the White House in 2024. The peril is unmistakable in Trump's increasingly authoritarian pronouncements, threats to jail opponents, and second-term plans to deploy the military for domestic law enforcement and to eviscerate and dominate the executive branch (Arnsdorf & Stein, 2023; Pengelly, 2023; Swan, 2022; Turner, 2023). Democratic institutions are at risk at least as long as Trump is a viable presidential candidate and the more so if he wins. At present, it looks like it will be up to ordinary voters to fend off the threat. That Trump is currently running neck and neck with Biden in horserace polls even though most Americans think him guilty of multiple felonies is not reassuring. If he does win – a real possibility given Biden's shaky standing with the public going into the election year – American democracy is likely to undergo stress tests even more severe than it experienced leading up to and through January 6.

Appendix: Survey Sources

Survey data used in this Element were acquired from survey reports and data accessed through the FiveThirtyEight website, the Roper Center, news reports, and the survey sponsors' websites. They are listed in the tables by the following numbers:

1 ABC News/Ipsos
2 ABC News/*Washington Post*
3 American Perspectives Survey
4 ANES 2022 Pilot Study
5 AP-NORC
6 Axios/Momentive
7 Bright Line Watch
8 CBS News and CBS News/YouGov
9 CNN
10 Echelon Insights
11 *Economist*/YouGov
12 Fox News
13 Gallup
14 Harvard Harris
15 Ipsos
16 Marquette University
17 Monmouth University
18 Morning Consult
19 Navigator Research
20 NBC News/*Wall Street Journal*
21 *New York Times*/Sienna
22 NPR/Marist
23 Pew Research Center
24 PRRI (Public Religion Research Institute)
25 Public Policy Polling
26 Quinnipiac University
27 Suffolk University
28 University of Massachusetts/YouGov
29 *Wall Street Journal*/GBAO
30 *Washington Post*/ University of Maryland
31 Yahoo News/YouGov

References

Some material in this Element was originally published by the author as "The 2022 Election: A Test of Democracy's Resilience and the Referendum Theory of Midterms," *Political Science Quarterly* 138(1):1–22, and "The Dimensions, Origins, and Consequences of Belief in Donald Trump's Big Lie," *Political Science Quarterly* 138(2):133–166.

Abramowitz, A. (2010). *The Disappearing Center: Engaged Citizens, Polarization, and American Democracy*. New Haven: Yale University Press.

Abramowitz, A. (2023). Donald Trump and the Disappearing Red Wave: Explaining Republican Underperformance in the 2022 Midterm Election. MPSA Annual Meeting, Chicago, April 13–16.

Abramowitz, A., & McCoy, J. (2018). United States: Racial Resentment, Negative Partisanship, and Polarization in Trump's America. *Annals of the American Academy of Arts and Sciences* 681(1):137–156.

Abramowitz, A., & Webster, S. (2018). Negative Partisanship: Why Americans Dislike Parties but Behave Like Rabid Partisans. *Political Psychology* 39 (S1):119–135.

Abrams, S., & Fiorina, M. (2015). Party Sorting: The Foundation of Polarized Politics. In J. Thurber, & A. Yoshinaka, eds., *American Gridlock: The Sources, Character, and Impact of Polarization*. New York: Cambridge University Press, pp. 113–129.

Aldrich, J., & 100+ cosigners. (2021). Statement of Concern: The Threats to American Democracy and the Need for National Voting and Election Administration Standards. New America Foundation, June 1, www.newamerica.org/political-reform/statements/statement-of-concern/.

Alfalo, M. (2022). Trump Vows Pardons, Government Apology to Capitol Rioters if Elected. *Washington Post*, September 1.

American National Election Studies. (2022a). ANES 2022 Pilot Study [dataset and documentation]. December 14, 2022 version, www.electionstudies.org.

American National Election Studies. (2022b). ANES Time Series Cumulative Data File [dataset and documentation]. September 16, 2022 version, www.electionstudies.org.

Anderson, C. (2019). *One Person, No Vote: How Voter Suppression Is Destroying Our Democracy*. New York: Bloomsbury.

Anderson, M. (2023). Antifa Didn't Storm the Capitol. Just Ask the Rioters. NPR, March 2, www.npr.org/2021/03/02/972564176/antifa-didnt-storm-the-capitol-just-ask-the-rioters.

Arnsdorf, I., & Stein, J. (2023). Trump Touts Authoritarian Vision for Second Term: "I Am Your Justice." *Washington Post*, April 21.

Arseneaux, K., & Truex, R. (2023). Donald Trump and the Lie. *Perspectives on Politics* 21(3):863–879.

Associated Press. (2021). Transcript of Trump's Speech at Rally before US Capitol Riot. January 13, https://apnews.com/article/election-2020-joe-biden-donald Associated Press-trump capitol-siege-media-e79eb5164613d6718e9f4502eb471f27.

Astor, M. (2022). Trump's Call for "Termination" of the Constitution Draws Rebukes. *New York Times*, December 4.

Bartels, L., & Carnes, N. (2023). House Republicans Were Rewarded for Supporting Donald Trump's "Stop the Steal" Efforts. *PNAS* 120(34): e2309072120.

Bauder, D. (2021). Riot? Insurrection? Words Matter in Describing Capitol Siege. *Associated Press*, February 23, https://apnews.com/article/donald-trump-capitol-siege-riots-media-8000ce7db2b176c1be386d945be5fd6a.

Bauder, D. (2022). What Is "Great Replacement Theory" and How Does It Fuel Racist Violence? PBS News Hour, May 16, www.pbs.org/newshour/politics/what-is-great-replacement-theory-and-how-does-it-fuel-racist-violence.

Behrmann, S., & Santucci, J. (2021). The Members of Congress Who Objected to Joe Biden's Electoral College Win amid Capitol Riot. *USA Today*, January 24.

Blake, A. (2023). Trump Repeatedly Evokes Threat of Violence over a Potential Indictment. *Washington Post*, March 23.

Brennan, M. (2023). Media Confidence in the US. Matches 2016 Record Low; Gallup Report, October 19, https://news.gallup.com/poll/512861/media-confidence-matches-2016-record-low.aspx.

Broockman, D., & Kalla, J. (2023). Selective Exposure and Partisan Echo Chambers in Partisan Television Consumption: Evidence from Linked Viewership, Administrative, and Survey Data. Preprint https://doi.org/10.31219/osf.io/b54s, https://osf.io/preprints/osf/b54sx.

Brooks, B., Lane, N., & Reid, T. (2020). Why Republican Voters Say There's "No Way in Hell" Trump Lost. Reuters, November 20, www.reuters.com/article/us-usa-election-trump-fraud-insight/why-republican-voters-say-theres-no-way-in-hell-trump-lost-idUSKBN2801D4.

Budrik, Z. (2020). Trump: Foreign Countries Will Print "Millions of Mail-In Ballots" in "Scandal of Our Times." *The Hill*, June 22.

Bullock, J., Gerber, A., Hill, S., & Huber, G. (2015). Partisan Bias in Factual Beliefs about Politics. *Quarterly Journal of Political Science* 10(4): 519–578.

Bump, P. (2021). What Donald Trump Has Said about the Capitol Rioters. *Washington Post*, July 22.

Calvin, J. (2023). Facing Legal Peril, Trump Calls on GOP to Rally Around Him as He Threatens Primary Challenges. *Los Angeles Times*, July 3.

Campbell, J. (2016). *Polarized: Making Sense of a Divide America*. Princeton: Princeton University Press.

Carson, J., & Jacobson, G. (2023). *The Politics of Congressional Elections*. 11th Ed. Lanham: Rowman and Littlefield.

Carson, J., & Ulrich, S. (2024). In the Shadow of Trump: The 2022 Midterm Elections. *Journal of Political Marketing*, forthcoming.

Carter, S. (2023). Donald Trump Praises Jan. 6 Rioters: "Great Patriots." *Newsweek*, January 14.

Cassidy, A. (2022). Far Too Little Vote Fraud to Tip Election to Trump, AP finds, AP News, December 14, https://apnews.com/article/voter-fraud-elec tion-2020-joe-biden-donald-trump-7fcb6f134e528fee8237c7601db3328f.

Chalfant, M. (2020). Trump: "The Only Way We're Going to Lose This Election Is if the Election Is Rigged." *The Hill*, August 17.

Cheney, K. (2020). Trump Calls on GOP State Legislatures to Overturn Election Results. *Politico*, November 21, www.politico.com/news/2020/11/21/trump-state-legislatures-overturn-election-results-439031.

Chinni, D. (2022). Both Parties Think the Other Will Destroy America, NBC News Poll Finds. NBC News, October 23, www.nbcnews.com/meet-the-press/both-parties-think-other-will-destroy-america-nbc-news-poll-n1300111.

Clifford, S., Kim, Y., & Sullivan, B. (2019). An Improved Question Format for Measuring Conspiracy Beliefs. *Public Opinion Quarterly* 83(4):690–722.

Cohn, N. (2023). Why Trump Is So Hard to Beat? *New York Times*, August 1.

Collins, P., & Eshbaugh-Soha, M. (2023). Trump's Latest Personal Attacks on Judges Could Further Weaken People's Declining Trust in American Rule of Law. Yahoo News, April 6, https://news.yahoo.com/trump-latest-personal-attacks-judges-120835683.html.

Corasaniti, N., Yourish, K., & Collins, K. (2022). How Trump's 2020 Election Lies Have Gripped State Legislatures. *New York Times*, May 22.

Costa, J. (2022). Trump Did Not Want to Tweet "Stay Peaceful" during January 6 riot, key former aide says. CNN, January 6, www.cnn.com/2022/01/06/politics/trump-tweet-january-6/.

Cox, D. (2021). After the Ballots Are Counted: Conspiracies, Political Violence, and American Exceptionalism. Survey Center on American Life, February 12, www.americansurveycenter.org/research/after-the-ballots-are-counted-con spiracies-political-violence-and-american-exceptionalism, 12 July 2022.

Cuthbert, L., & Theodoridis, A. (2022). Do Republicans Really Believe Trump Won the 2020 Election? Our Research Suggests that They Do. *Washington Post*, January 7.

Dale, D. (2022). 10 Trump Election Lies His Own Officials Called False. CNN, June 16, www.cnn.com/2022/06/16/politics/fact-check-trump-officials-testi mony-debunking-election-lies/index.html.

Danforth, J., Ginsberg, B., Griffith, T., et al. (2022). Lost, Not Stolen: The Conservative Case that Trump Lost and Biden Won the 2020 Presidential Election, https://lostnotstolen.org//wp-content/uploads/2022/07/Lost-Not-Stolen-The-Conservative-Case-that-Trump-Lost-and-Biden-Won-the-2020-Presidential-Election-July-2022.pdf, 25 July 2022.

Dawsey, J., & Sonmez, F. (2022). "Legitimate Political Discourse": Three Words about Jan. 6 Spar Rift among Republicans. *Washington Post*, February 22.

Day, J., Khan, A., & Loadenthal, M. (2022). Elected Officials Are Being Threatened and Attacked. We're Tracking That. *Washington Post*, November 9.

Deane, C., & Gramlich, J. (2020). 2020 Election Reveals Two Broad Voting Coalitions Fundamentally at Odds. Pew Research Center, November 6.

Ding, X., Horning, M., & Rho, E. (2020). Same Words, Different Meanings: Semantic Polarization in Broadcast Media Language Forecasts Polarity in Online Public Discourse, Proceedings of the Seventeenth International AAAI Conference on Web and Social Media (ICWSM2023)161.

Edsall, T. (2023). Why Millions Think It Is Trump Who Cannot Tell a Lie. *New York Times*, January 19.

Egan, P. (2023). "Hear No Evil or Follow the Leader: Why Trump's Voters Are Inured to Accounts of His Most Egregious Words and Deeds. Paper presented at the 2023 APSA Annual Meeting, Los Angeles, California, August 31–September 3.

Ellison, S., Farhi, P., & Barr, J. (2023). Fox News Feared Losing Viewers by Airing Truth about Election, Documents Show. *Washington Post*, February 17.

Elving, R. (2022). Imagine Another American Civil War, but This Time in Every State. NPR, January 11, www.npr.org/2022/01/11/1071082955/imagine-another-american-civil-war-but-this-time-in-every-state.

Enders, A., Klopstad, C., Stoler, J., & Uscinski, J. (2022). How Anti-social Personality Traits and Anti-establishment Views Promote Beliefs in Election Fraud, QAnon, and COVID-19 Conspiracy Theories and Misinformation. *Political Behavior* 51(2):247–259.

Fahey, J. (2022). The Big Lie: Expressive Responding and Misperceptions in the United States. *Journal of Experimental Political Science* 10(2):267–278. https://doi.org/10.1017/XPS.2022.33.

Feuer, A. (2023a). Two Years Later, Prosecution of Jan. 6 Rioters Continues to Grow. *New York Times*, January 6.

Feuer, A. (2023b). In Miami, the Only Violence from Trump Supporters Was Rhetorical. *New York Times*, June 13.

Fields, G. (2023). Presidential Centers from Hoover to Bush and Obama Unite to Warn of Fragile State of US Democracy. Associated Press, September 7, https://apnews.com/article/united-states-democracy-presidents-threats-joint-statement-5530a89df2c41d58a22961f63fb0e6ff. \

Fingerhut, H. (2018). Why Do People Belong to a Party? Negative Views of the Opposing Party Are a Major Factor. Pew Research Report, March 29.

Folkenflik, D. (2023). Off the Air, Fox News Stars Blasted the Election Fraud Claims. NPR, February 16, www.npr.org/2023/02/16/1157558299/fox-news-stars-false-claims-trump-election-2020.

Fortinsky, S. (2022). Trump Says He Wanted Pence to Overturn the 2020 Election and Falsely Claims It Was Vice President's "Right." CNN, January 31, www.cnn.com/2022/01/30/politics/trump-pence-2020-election/index.html.

Goodwin, L. (2022). A Wave of Red Criticism Crashes into Donald Trump after Midterm Loss. *Washington Post*, November 11.

Graham, M., & Coppock, A. (2021). Asking about Attitude Change. *Public Opinion Quarterly* 85(1):26–53.

Graham, M., & Svolik, M. (2020). Democracy in America? Partisanship, Polarization, and the Robustness of Support for Democracy in the United States. *American Political Science Review* 114(2):392–409.

Graham, M., & Yair, O. (2023). Expressive Responding and Trump's Big Lie. *Political Behavior*, July 26, https://doi.org/10.1007/s11109-023-09875-w.

Gramlich, J. (2022). A Look Back at Americans' Reactions to the Jan. 6 Riot at the U.S. Capitol. Pew Research Center, January 4.

Grofman, B., & Cervas, J. (2023). Statistical Fallacies in Claims about 'Massive and Widespread Fraud' in the 2020 Presidential Election: Examining Claims Based on Aggregate Election Results. *Statistics and Public Policy* 11(1):1–36. www.tandfonline.com/loi/uspp20.

Hajnal, Z., Lajevardi, N., & Nielson, N. (2017). Voter Identification Laws and the Suppression of Minority Votes. *Journal of Politics* 79(2):363–379.

Harris, J. (2020). Democrats Look at Trump Voters and Wonder, "What the Hell Is Your Problem?" *Politico*, November 4, www.politico.com/news/magazine/2020/11/04/democrats-trump-voters-434100.

Hasen, R. (2022). Identifying and Minimizing the Risk of Election Subversion and Stolen Elections in the Contemporary United States. *Harvard Law Review Forum* 135:265–301.

Hassan, S. (2020). *The Cult of Trump*. New York: The Free Press.

Hetherington, M., & Weiler, J. (2009). *Authoritarianism and Polarization in American Politics*. Cambridge: Cambridge University Press.

Hernandez, S., & Lash, N. (2023). Fortune 500 Companies Have Given Millions to Election Deniers since Jan. 6. ProPublica, July 9, https://projects.propublica.org/fortune-500-company-election-deniers-jan-6/.

Hooghe, M., & Dassonnevelle, R. (2018). Explaining the Trump Vote: The Effect of Racist Resentment and Anti-immigrant Sentiments. *PS: Political Science and Politics*, 51(3):528–534.

Huff, I. (2022). QAnon Beliefs Have Increased since 2021 as Americans Are Less Likely to Reject Conspiracies. PRRI, June 24, www.prri.org/spotlight/qanon-beliefs-have-increased-since-2021-as-americans-are-less-likely-to-reject-conspiracies/.

Hulse, C., & Fandos, N. (2021). McConnell, Denouncing Trump after Voting to Acquit, Says His Hands Were Tied. *New York Times*, February 17.

Itkowitz, C. (2021). Trump Falsely Claims Jan. 6 Rioters Were "Hugging and Kissing" Police. *Washington Post*, March 26.

Itkowitz, C. (2022). GOP Turns to False Insinuations of LGBTQ Grooming against Democrats. *Washington Post*, April 22.

Iyengar, S., & Krupenkin, M. (2018). Partisanship as Social Identity; Implications for the Study of Party Polarization. *The Forum* 16(1):23–45.

Jackson, C. (2022). Very Few Americans Believe Political Violence Is Acceptable. Ipsos, August 22, www.ipsos.com/en-us/very-few-americans-believe-political-violence-acceptable.

Jacobson, G. (2013). Partisan Polarization in American Politics: A Background Paper. *Presidential Studies Quarterly* 43(4):688–708.

Jacobson, G. (2017). The Triumph of Polarized Partisanship: Donald Trump's Improbable Victory in 2016. *Political Science Quarterly* 132(2):1–34.

Jacobson, G. (2019a). Money and Mobilization in the 2018 Congressional Elections. Paper delivered at Partisanship Reconsidered: A Conference to Honor David Magleby. Brigham Young University, June 6–8.

Jacobson, G. (2019b). Extreme Referendum: Donald Trump and the 2018 Midterm Elections. *Political Science Quarterly* 134(1):1–30.

Jacobson, G. (2021a). Donald Trump's Big Lie and the Future of the Republican Party. *Presidential Studies Quarterly* 51(2):273–289.

Jacobson, G. (2021b). Driven to Extremes: Donald Trump's Extraordinary Impact on the 2020 Elections. *Presidential Studies Quarterly* 51(3):492–521.

Jacobson, G. (2023a). The 2022 Elections: A Test of Democracy's Resilience and the Referendum Theory of Midterms. *Political Science Quarterly* 138(1):1–22.

Jacobson, G. (2023b). The Dimensions, Origins, and Consequences of Belief in Donald Trump's Big Lie. *Political Science Quarterly* 138(2): 133–166.

Jarvie, J. (2020). As Georgia GOP Feuds over Trump Loss, Might It Hurt Party Turnout for Senate Runoffs? *Los Angeles Times*, November 23.

Johnson, T., & Feldman, M. (2020). The New Voter Suppression. Brennan Center for Justice, www.brennancenter.org/our-work/research-reports/new-voter-suppression.

Jones, J. (2022). Government Agency Ratings: CIA, FBI UP; Federal Reserve Down. Gallup Report, October 5, https://news.gallup.com/poll/402464/government-agency-ratings-cia-fbi-federal-reserve-down.aspx.

Jurkowitz, M., Mitchell, A., Shearer, E., & Walker, M. (2020). U.S. Media Polarization and the 2020 Election: A Nation Divided. Pew Research Center, January 24.

Kalmoe, N., & Mason, L. (2022). *Radical American Partisanship: Mapping Violent Hostility, Its Causes, and the Consequences for Democracy.* Chicago: University of Chicago Press.

Karni, A. (2022). Racist Attack Spotlights Stefanik's Echo of Replacement Theory. *New York Times*, May 16.

Kessler, B. (2016). Donald Trump's Bogus Claim that Millions of People Voted Illegally for Hilary Clinton. *Washington Post*, November 17.

Kinder, D., & Sanders, L. (1996). *Divided by Color: Racial Politics and Democratic Ideals.* Chicago: University of Chicago Press.

Klienfeld, R. (2022). The Rise in Political Violence in the United States and Damage to Our Democracy. Carnegie Endowment for International Peace, March 31, https://carnegieendowment.org/2022/03/31/rise-in-political-violence-in-united-states-and-damage-to-our-democracy-pub-87584.

Kunda, Z. (1990). The Case for Motivated Reasoning. *Psychological Bulletin* 108(3):480–498.

Layne, N. (2023). Trump Magnifies Attacks on Justice Department after His Indictment. Reuters, June 12, www.reuters.com/world/us/trump-magnifies-attacks-justice-department-post-charges-speech-2023-06-10/.

Lebo, M., & Cassino, D. (2007). The Aggregated Consequences of Motivated Reasoning and the Dynamics of Partisan Presidential Approval. *Political Psychology* 28(6):719–746.

Lee, J. (2022). Did Trump Tell Supporters to Storm the US Capitol on Jan. 6, 2021? *Snopes*, June 22, www.snopes.com/news/2022/06/22/trump-hearings-committee/.

Lelkes, Y. (2016). Mass Polarization: Manifestations and Measurements. *Public Opinion Quarterly* 80(S1):392–410.

Leonhardt, D. (2022). "A Crisis Coming": The Twin Threats to American Democracy. *New York Times*, September 17.

Levendusky, M. (2009). *The Partisan Sort: How Liberals Became Democrats and Conservatives Became Republicans*. Chicago: University of Chicago Press.

Levendusky, M., Patterson, S., Margolis, M., et al. (2023). The Long Shadow of The Big Lie: How Beliefs about the Legitimacy of the 2020 Election Spill Over onto Future Elections. Manuscript, University of Pennsylvania, July 12.

Levitsky, S., & Ziblatt, D. (2023). *Tyranny of the Minority: Why American Democracy Reached the Breaking Point*. New York: Crown.

Lewis, T. (2021). The "Shared Psychosis" of Donald Trump and His Loyalists. *Scientific American*, January 11, www.scientificamerican.com/article/the-shared-psychosis-of-donald-trump-and-his-loyalists/.

Lodge, M., & Tabor, C. (2013). *The Rationalizing Voter*. New York: Cambridge.

Longwell, S. (2022). Trump Supporters Explain Why They Believe the Big Lie. *The Atlantic*, April 18, www.theatlantic.com/ideas/archive/2022/04/trump-voters-big-lie-stolen-election/629572/.

Lopez, J., & Hillygus, D. (2018). Why So Serious?: Survey Trolls and Misinformation. SSRN, March 14, https://ssrn.com/abstract=3131087.

Malka, A., & Adelman, M. (2022). Expressive Survey Responding: A Closer Look at the Evidence and Its Implications for American Democracy. *Perspectives on Politics* 21(4):1198–1209.

Malzahn, J., & Hall, A. (2023). Election-Denying Republican Candidates Underperformed in the 2022 Midterms. Stanford Business School, Working Paper No. 4076, www.gsb.stanford.edu/faculty-research/working-papers/election-denying-republican-candidates-underperformed-2022-midterms.

Marcotte, A. (2023). New Trump Poll Proves Obama and Clinton Were Right: The GOP Base Are Deplorable, Bitter Clingers. *Salon*, August 22, www.msn.com/en-us/news/politics/new-trump-poll-proves-obama-and-clinton-were-right-the-gop-base-are-deplorable-bitter-clingers/.

Martherus, J., Martinez, A., Piff, P., & Theororidis, A. (2021). Party Animals? Extreme Partisan Polarization and Dehumanization. *Political Behavior* 43:517–540.

McCarthy, B. (2021). Tucker Carlson's "Patriot Purge" Film on Jan. 6 is Full of Falsehoods, Conspiracy Theories. Politifact, November 5, www.politifact.com/article/2021/nov/05/tucker-carlsons-patriot-purge-film-jan-6-full-fals/.

McClosky, H., & Brill, A. (1983). *Dimensions of Tolerance: What Americans Think about Civil Liberties*. New York: Russell Sage Foundation.

Mir, A. (2020). *Postjournalism and the Death of Newspapers. The Media after Trump: Manufacturing Anger and Polarization.* Amazon (independently published).

Montanaro, D. (2022). Trump Escalates Racist Rhetoric and Plays on White Grievance at Recent Rallies. NPR, February 2, www.npr.org/2022/02/01/ 1077166847/trump-escalates-racist-rhetoric-plays-on-white-grievance-at-recent-rallies.

Moritz, J. (2023). Why These CT Experts Think Trump's Supporters Continue to Stick by Him Despite Indictments. CT Insider, August 26, www.ctinsider .com/politics/article/ct-donald-trump-indictment-mug-shot-uconn-experts-18306406.php.

Naylor, B. (2021). Read Trump's Jan. 6 Speech, A Key Part of Impeachment Trial. NPR, February 10, www.npr.org/2021/02/10/966396848/read-trumps-jan-6-speech-a-key-part-of-impeachment-trial.

NPR Staff. (2024). The Jan. 6 Attack: The Cases behind the Biggest Criminal Investigation in U.S. History. September 18, www.npr.org/2021/02/09/ 965472049/the-capitol-siege-the-arrested-and-their-stories.

Nyhan, B. (2021). Why the Backfire Effect Does Not Explain the Durability of Political Misperceptions. PNAS 118(15), https://doi.org/10.1073/pnas.19124 40117.

Paleologos, D. (2021). Move over Fox News, Trump Voters Are Shifting toward Newsmax, OANN. *USA Today*, February 21.

Pape, R. (2022a). *American Face of Insurrection: Analysis of Individuals Charged with Storming the U.S. Capitol on January 6, 2021.* University of Chicago Project on Security and Threats.

Pape, R. (2022b). *"Patriotic Counter-Revolution": The Political Mindset that Stormed the Capitol.* University of Chicago Project on Security and Threats.

Peffley, M., & Rohrschneider, R. (2009). Elite Beliefs and the Theory of Democratic Elitism. In R. Dalton, & H.-D. Klingeman, eds., *The Oxford Handbook of Political Behavior.* Oxford: Oxford University Press, pp. 65–79.

Pengelly, M. (2023). Sarah Palin Says US Civil War "Is Going to Happen" over Trump Prosecutions. *The Guardian*, August 25, www.theguardian.com/us-news/2023/aug/25/sarah-palin-us-civil-war-donald-trump-prosecutions.

Peters, J., & Feuer, A. (2023). The Case that Could Be Fox's Next Dominion. *New York Times*, July 10.

Peters, J., & Robertson, K. (2023). Fox Stars Privately Expressed Disbelief about Election Fraud Claims. "Crazy Stuff." *New York Times*, April 24.

Peterson, E., & Iyengar, S. (2021). Partisan Gaps in Political Information and Information-Seeking Behavior. *American Journal of Political Science* 65(1):133–147.

Pew Research Center. (2021). Biden Begins Presidency with Positive Ratings; Trump Departs with Lowest-Ever Job Mark. Research Report, January 15.

Piper, J. (2023). Most GOP Candidates Say They Will Support Trump Again – Even if He Is Convicted. *Politico*, August 23, www.politico.com/news/2023/08/23/trump-indictment-gop-debate-00112661.

PRRI Staff. (2021). Understanding QAnon's Connection to American Politics, Religion, and Media Consumption. May 27, www.prri.org/research/qanon-conspiracy-american-politics-report/.

Raju, J., Mattingly, P., Zeleny, J., Acosta, J., & Collins, K. (2021). McConnell Believes Impeachment Push Will Help Rid Trump from the GOP, but Not Said if He Will Vote to Convict. CNN, January 13, www.cnn.com/2021/01/12/politics/mcconnell-impeachment-trump-capitol-riot/index.html.

Reich, R. (2023). Trump Is Undermining the Entire US Judicial System with Another Big Lie. *The Guardian*, August 16, www.theguardian.com/commentisfree/2023/aug/16/donald-trump-big-lie-fulton-county-georgia-indictment.

Rhodes, J., La Raja, R., Nteta, T., & Theodoridis, A. (2022). Martin Luther King Jr. Was Right. Racism and Opposition to Democracy Are Linked, Our Research Finds. *Washington Post*, January 17.

Richards, Z. (2022). McCarthy Said He Would Urge Trump to Resign after Jan. 6, New Audio Reveals. NBC News, April 22, www.nbcnews.com/politics/donald-trump/mccarthy-said-urge-trump-resign-jan-6-new-audio-reveals-rcna25509.

Rissman, K. (2023). Trump Causes Confusion by Sharing Meme Calling Jan 6 a "Government Staged Riot" Even Though He Was in Power. Yahoo News, July 24, https://news.yahoo.com/trump-causes-confusion-sharing-meme-142311854.html.

Romano, A. (2022). Poll: 61% of Trump Voters Agree with the Idea Behind "Great Replacement" Conspiracy Theory. Yahoo News, May 24, https://news.yahoo.com/hed-poll-61-of-trump-voters-agree-with-idea-behind-great-replacement-conspiracy-theory-090004062.html.

Rosenberg, M. (2020). Republican Voters Take a Radical Conspiracy Theory Mainstream. *New York Times*, November 20.

Ross, R., & Levy, H. (2023). Expressive Responding in Support of Donald Trump: An Extended Replication of Schaffner and Luks (2018). *Collabra: Psychology* 9(1):68054, https://online.ucpress.edu/collabra/article/9/1/68054/195155/Expressive-Responding-in-Support-of-Donald-Trump.

Rutenberg, J., Schmidt, M., & Peters, J. (2023). Missteps and Miscalculations: Inside Fox's Legal and Business Debacle. *New York Times*, June 1.

Sagal, P. (2023). The End Will Come for the Cult of MAGA. *The Atlantic*, August 20, www.theatlantic.com/ideas/archive/2023/08/trumpism-maga-cult-republican-voters-indoctrination/675173/.

Schaffner, B., & Luks, S. (2018). Misinformation or Expressive Responding? What an Inauguration Crowd Can Tell Us about the Source of Political Misinformation in Surveys. *Public Opinion Quarterly* 82(1):135–147.

Schmidt, M., Feuer, A., Haberman, M., & Goldman, A. (2023a). Trump Supporters' Violent Rhetoric in His Defense Disturbs Experts. *New York Times*, June 14.

Schmidt, M., Goldman, A., Feuer, A., Haberman, M., & Thrush, G. (2023b). As Trump Prosecutions Move Forward, Threats and Concerns Increase. *New York Times*, September 24.

Scott, E. (2019). Trump's Most Recent Insulting – and Violent – Language Is Often Reserved for Immigrants. *Washington Post*, October 2.

Sebastian, M. (2017). 30 Times Donald Trump Has Been Completely Insulting to Women. *Cosmopolitan*, June 19.

Serwer, A. (2018). Cruelty Is the Point. *The Atlantic*, October 3, www.theatlantic.com/ideas/archive/2018/10/the-cruelty-is-the-point/572104/.

Serwer, A. (2020). "If You Didn't Vote for Trump, Your Vote Is Fraudulent." *The Atlantic*, December 10, www.theatlantic.com/ideas/archive/2020/12/voter-fraud/617354/.

Sides, J., Tausanovitch, C., & Vavreck, L. (2022). *The Bitter End: The 2020 Presidential Campaign and the Challenge to American Democracy.* Princeton: Princeton University press.

Sides, J., Tesler, M., & Vavreck, L. (2018). *Identity Crisis: The 2016 Presidential Campaign and the Battle for the Meaning of America.* Princeton: Princeton University Press.

Silverman, E., & Allam, H. (2023). Among MAGA Extremists, Trump Charges Draw Big Talk, Small Crowds. *Washington Post*, August 3.

Smith, D. (2023). Biden Impeachment Effort "Eight Months of Abject Failure," Watchdog Report Says. *The Guardian*, September 11, www.theguardian.com/us-news/2023/sep/11/biden-impeachment-inquiry-abject-failure-report.

Smith, T. (2022). They Believe in Trump's "Big Lie." Here's Why It's Been So Hard to Dispel. NPR, January 5, www.npr.org/2022/01/05/1070362852/trump-big-lie-election-jan-6-families.

Sommer, W. (2023). *Trust the Plan: The Rise of QAnon and the Conspiracy That Unhinged America.* New York: Harper.

Stanley-Becker, I. (2023). Jeffrey Clark Is GOP Star after Trying to Use DOJ to Overturn Election. *Washington Post*, August 3.

Stouffer, S. (1955). *Communism, Conformity and Civil Liberties*. New York: Doubleday.

Survey Center on American Life. (2021). The January 2021 American Perspectives Survey, January 21–30, www.americansurveycenter.org/down load/jan-2021-american-perspectives-survey/.

Swan, J. (2022). A Radical Plan for Trump's Second Term. *Axios*, July 22, www.axios.com/2022/07/22/trump-2025-radical-plan-second-term.

Tausanovitch, C., & Vavreck, L. (2020). Democracy Fund + UCLA Nationscape, October 10– 17, 2019 (version 20200131).

Tesler, M. (2016). Views about Race Mattered More in Electing Trump than in Electing Obama. *Washington Post*, November 22.

Thompson, S. (2022). QAnon Candidates Aren't Thriving, but Some of Their Ideas Are. *New York Times*, July 25.

Thompson-DeVeaux, A. (2022). Why Many Americans Might Be Increasingly Accepting of Political Violence. FiveThirtyEight, January 6, https://fivethir tyeight.com/features/why-many-americans-might-be-increasingly-accept ing-of-political-violence/.

Tully-McManus, K. (2020). QAnon Goes to Washington: Two Supporters Win Seats in Congress. *Roll Call*, November 5, https://rollcall.com/2020/11/05/ qanon-goes-to-washington-two-supporters-win-seats-in-congress/.

Turner, A. (2023). 14 Promises Donald Trump Has Made in His Campaign for a Second Term. CNN, July 8, www.cnn.com/2023/07/08/politics/trump-cam paign-promises/index.html.

U. S. House of Representatives. (2022). *Final Report of the Select Committee to Investigate the January 6th Attack on the United States Capitol* (H.R. Rep. No. 117–613), 117th Cong., 2nd Sess., December 22, 2022.

Uscinski, J., & Parent, J. (2014). *American Conspiracy Theories*. New York: Oxford.

Vachon, N. (2023). Corporate PACS Have Given More Than $50 Million to Election Objectors since Jan. 6. *The American Independent*, January 11, https://americanindependent.com/corporate-pacs-donate-50-million-elec tion-deniers-jan-6/.

Walter, B. (2022). Why Should We Worry that the U.S. Could Become an 'Anocracy' Again? Because of the Threat of Civil War. *Washington Post*, January 24.

Westwood, S., Grimmer, J., Tyler, M., & Nall, C. (2022). Current Research Overstates American Support for Political Violence. PNAS 119(12): e2116870119.

Weyland, K. (2020). Populism's Threat to Democracy: Comparative Lessons for the United States. *Perspectives on Politics* 18(2):389–406.

Wolf, J. (2023). Trump Shared Article: Republicans Will be Enslaved, Outlawed if Trump Loses. MSNBC, September 12, www.msn.com/en-us/news/politics/trump-shared-article-republicans-will-be-enslaved-outlawed-if-trump-loses/ar-AA1gCLZ6.

Yang, M. (2023). Compare the Election-Fraud Claims Fox News Aired with What Its Stars Knew. NPR, February 18, www.npr.org/2023/02/18/1157972219/fox-news-election-fraud-claims-vs-what-they-knew.

Younis, M. (2019). FBI's Positive Job Ratings Steady among Americans. Gallup Report, May 10.

Cambridge Elements ☰

American Politics

Frances E. Lee
Princeton University

Frances E. Lee is Professor of Politics at the Woodrow Wilson School of Princeton University. She is author of *Insecure Majorities: Congress and the Perpetual Campaign* (2016), *Beyond Ideology: Politics, Principles and Partisanship in the U.S. Senate* (2009), and coauthor of *Sizing Up the Senate: The Unequal Consequences of Equal Representation* (1999).

Advisory Board

About the Series

The Cambridge Elements Series in American Politics publishes authoritative contributions on American politics. Emphasizing works that address big, topical questions within the American political landscape, the series is open to all branches of the subfield and actively welcomes works that bridge subject domains. It publishes both original new research on topics likely to be of interest to a broad audience and state-of-the-art synthesis and reconsideration pieces that address salient questions and incorporate new data and cases to inform arguments.

Cambridge Elements ☰

American Politics

Elements in the Series

9 781009 495370